SURVIVAL
THAI

SURVIVAL THAI

How to communicate without fuss or fear INSTANTLY!

by THOMAS LAMOSSE
& JINTANA RATTANAKHEMAKORN

TUTTLE Publishing

Tokyo | Rutland, Vermont | Singapore

CONTENTS

PART 3 Situations, Making Plans, Sightseeing

PART 4 Exploring Thailand

PART 5 Vocabulary List

INTRODUCTION

Thai: Think Simple Sentences

Thai is unlike English in many ways. You may be afraid of Thai at first because of the tones and many odd sounds we do not have in the English language but Thai sentences are very easy.

Most Thai people do not expect a foreigner to be able to speak Thai language. However, they are always surprised if you can say a few sentences. With a fair amount of survival phrases, you will find it a lot easier to get discount at the markets, to order food and to travel around Thailand.

Note: Please read through the rest of this Introduction to help you understand that Thai is a tonal language and if you say a word correctly but with the wrong tone you will *not* be understood. You need this essential background on tones and odd character sounds in order to communicate.

Sound system and pronunciation guide

In this introductory section, you will find guidelines for the correct pronunciation of each Thai vowel and consonant. Throughout the book, each time a Thai word or phrase is used, romanized pronunciation is presented in parenthesis (....), and also a hyphen mark "–" is included for a syllable break within a multi-syllable word.

THAI CONSONANTS

There are 44 consonant characters in Thai representing 20 consonant sounds.

Consonant Form	Consonant Sound	Sounds like	Example
ก	k	/g/ as in go	กิน _kin_
ข ค ฆ	kh	/k/ as in kid	ขา _khǎa_
ง	ng	/ng/ as in singing	งู _ngou_
จ	j	/j/ as in jet	จาน _jaan_
ฉ ช ฌ	ch	/ch/ as in check	ฉัน _chǎn_
ซ ศ ษ ส	s	/s/ as in send	สวย _sǔay_
ญ ย	y	/y/ as in you	ยา _yaa_

Consonant Form	Consonant Sound	Sounds like	Example
ฏ ด	d	/d/ as in do	เดิน _doen_
ฏ ต	t	/t/ as in stamp	เต้น _tên_
ฐ ฑ ฒ ถ ท ธ	th	/t/ as in touch	ไทย _thai_
ณ น	n	/n/ as in nine	น้ำ _nám_
บ	b	/b/ as in boy	บ้าน _bâan_
ป	p	/p/ as in spy	ไป _pai_
ผ พ ภ	ph	/p/ as in pot	พ่อ _phâw_
ฝ ฟ	f	/f/ as in fine	ฟัน _fan_
ม	m	/m/ as in make	แมว _maew_
ร	r	/r/ as in rat	เรียน _rian_
ล ฬ	l	/l/ as in lot	ลอง _lawng_
ว	w	/w/ as in wine	วัด _wát_
ห ฮ	h	/h/ as in hand	หิว _hǐw_

THAI VOWELS

There are 18 single vowels in Thai. Thai vowels have two "sounds"; **short** and **long**.

1. Short vowels

There are nine "short" vowels:

Vowel Form	Vowel Sound	Sounds like	Example
-ะ	a	/a/ as in b<u>u</u>t	จะ _jà_
-ิ	i	/i/ as in h<u>i</u>t	สิ _sì_
-ึ	ue	/ue/ as in list<u>e</u>n	รึ _rúe_
-ุ	u	/u/ as in p<u>u</u>t	ดุ _dù_
เ-ะ	e	/e/ as in m<u>e</u>t	เตะ _tè_
แ-ะ	ae	/ae/ as in h<u>a</u>t	แตะ _láe_
โ-ะ	o	/o/ as in <u>o</u>nly	โปะ _pò_
เ-าะ	aw	/aw/ as in h<u>o</u>t	เกาะ _kàw_
เ-อะ	er	/er/ as in <u>uh</u>	เถอะ _thòe_

2. Long vowels

Each of the short vowels above has its long counterpart:

Vowel Form	Vowel Sound	Sounds like	Example
-า	*aa*	/aa/ as in f<u>a</u>r	ชา *ch<u>aa</u>*
◌ี	*ii*	/ii/ as in <u>tea</u>	ดี *d<u>ii</u>*
◌ื	*ue*	/ue/ as in <u>umm</u>	มือ *m<u>ue</u>*
◌ู	*ou*	/ou/ as in c<u>ou</u>ld	ปู *p<u>ou</u>*
เ-	*e*	/e/ as in t<u>e</u>st	เท *th<u>e</u>*
แ-	*ae*	/ae/ as in c<u>a</u>n	แจ *j<u>ae</u>*
โ-	*o*	/o/ as in t<u>o</u>ne	โม *m<u>o</u>*
-อ	*aw*	/aw/ as in s<u>aw</u>	ขอ *kh<u>ăw</u>*
เ-อ	*er*	/er/ as in h<u>er</u>	เจอ *j<u>er</u>*

Note: The letter "อ" in Thai can be pronounced *a*, *e*, *i*, *o*, or *u*, depending on where it appears. For example:

อ่าน *àan*	/a/ as in <u>a</u>t
เอ็ด *èt*	/e/ as in <u>e</u>gg
อิ่ม *ìm*	/i/ as in <u>i</u>t
อ้วน *oûan*	/o/ as in <u>o</u>n
อุ่น *ùn*	/u/ as in <u>u</u>p

ENDING

When these consonants appear at the end of a word, they are not voiced aloud.

Consonant sound	Sounds like	Consonant form (Thai word)
k	/g/ as in ba<u>g</u>	จาก *jàa<u>k</u>*
t	/d/ as in clou<u>d</u>	พูด *phôu<u>t</u>*
p	/b/ as in ca<u>b</u>	ครับ *khrá<u>p</u>*
ng	/ng/ as in ha<u>ng</u>	ลอง *law<u>ng</u>*
n	/n/ as in fa<u>n</u>	กิน *ki<u>n</u>*
m	/m/ as in ru<u>m</u>	ส้ม *sô<u>m</u>*
y	/y/ as in dr<u>y</u>	ขาย *khǎa<u>y</u>*
w	/w/ as in co<u>w</u>	แล้ว *láe<u>w</u>*

TONES

Thai has only five distinctive tones; mid, low, falling, high, and rising. They all carry tone marks except for mid-level tones. The pitch of a particular word changes its meaning.

Tone mark	Tone level	Symbol	Example	Meaning
No mark	mid	−	คา *khaa*	to get stuck
่	low	`	ข่า *khàa*	Galanga (a plant in the ginger family)
้	falling	^	ข้า *khâa*	I, slave, servant
๊	high	´	ค้า *kháa*	trade
๋	rising	ˇ	ขา *khǎa*	leg

How a Thai sentence works

Thai grammar is very simple when compared with English or other European languages. Basic Thai word order is regular with every sentence structured by "subject-verb-object" order like English. But most Thai words are not modified or conjugated for tense, person, possession, singular or plural, gender, or subject-verb agreement. Also, determiners such as *a*, *an*, or *the* are not used.

POLITE PARTICLES (*KHÁ/KHÂ/KHRÁP*)

These particles are often used to end a sentence in order to make an utterance sound very polite and respectful, as well as vary the level of formality.

- The word *khâ* (for women) is used for statements, commands, and also used alone as a polite way to answer "yes."
- *khá* (for women) is used at the end of a question.
- *khráp* is a neutral ending for men to use in any situation.

PART ONE
Getting Started

Common Expressions and Phrases

Hello (to female speakers)	*(sà-wàt-dii khâ)*	สวัสดีค่ะ
Hello (to male speakers)	*(sà-wàt-dii khráp)*	สวัสดีครับ
I, me (female speakers)	*(chăn)*	ฉัน
I, me (male speakers)	*(phŏm)*	ผม
name	*(chûe)*	ชื่อ

▶ **My name is....**
(chăn chûe/phŏm chûe)
ฉัน ชื่อ.../ผม ชื่อ...

▶ **How are you?**
(sà-baay-dii mái)
สบายดีไหม

▶ **I am fine.**
   (sà-baay-dii)
   สบายดี

▶ **Thank you.**
   (khàwp-khun)
   ขอบคุณ

▶ **Excuse me. / I am sorry.**
   (khăw-thôt)
   ขอโทษ

▶ **You're welcome. / That's all right.**
   (mâi-pen-rai)
   ไม่เป็นไร

▶ **I don't understand.**
   (mâi-khâo-jai)
   ไม่เข้าใจ

▶ **I don't know.**
   (mâi-róu)
   ไม่รู้

▶ **Speak slowly, please.**
   (phôut cháa-cháa)
   พูดช้า ๆ

▶ **I'd like… / May I have…?** (for request)
(khăw…)
ขอ…

▶ **I am a vegetarian.**
(chăn/phŏm kin jay)
ฉัน/ผม กินเจ

▶ **I am hungry.**
(chăn/phŏm hĭw)
ฉัน/ผม หิว

▶ **I am thirsty.**
(chăn/phŏm hĭw nám)
ฉัน/ผม หิวน้ำ

▶ **I am already full.**
(chăn/phŏm ìm láew)
ฉัน/ผม อิ่มแล้ว

▶ **Where is the bathroom?**
(hâwng-nám yóu thîi-năi)
ห้องน้ำอยู่ที่ไหน

▶ **How much is it?**
(thâo-rài)
เท่าไร

▶ **Can you lower the price?**
(lót dâi-mái)
ลดได้ไหม

▶ **Can you help me?**
(chûay chǎn/phǒm dâi-mái)
ช่วย ฉัน/ผม ได้ไหม

▶ **What time is it?**
(kìi-mong)
กี่โมง

▶ **Can you speak English?**
(khun phôut phaa-sǎa-ang-krìt dâi-mái)
คุณพูดภาษาอังกฤษได้ไหม

▶ **What is this?**
(nîi à-rai)
นี่อะไร

▶ **How do you say this in Thai?**
(phaa-sǎa-thai phôut yang-ngai)
ภาษาไทยพูดยังไง

▶ **I'm feeling sick.**
(chǎn/phǒm mâi sà-baay)
ฉัน/ผม ไม่สบาย

▶ **I am allergic to …**
(chăn/phŏm-pháe …)
ฉัน/ผม แพ้ …

Note: For many phrases, you will see options, indicated by a slash "/." This is because in Thai you may say something differently depending on whether the speaker is male or female.

Common Actions and Movements

Go	*(pai)*	ไป
Go together	*(pai-dûay)*	ไปด้วย
Come	*(maa)*	มา
Arrive	*(thŭeng)*	ถึง
Fast	*(rew)*	เร็ว
Slow	*(cháa)*	ช้า
Walk	*(dern)*	เดิน
Run	*(wîng)*	วิ่ง
Sit	*(nâng)*	นั่ง
Stand	*(yuen)*	ยืน
Drive	*(khàp)*	ขับ
Sleep	*(nawn)*	นอน
Think	*(khít)*	คิด
Swim	*(wâay-nám)*	ว่ายน้ำ

Play	*(lên)*	เล่น
Throw	*(yon)*	โยน
Kick	*(tè)*	เตะ
Punch	*(tàwy)*	ต่อย
Bite	*(gàt)*	กัด
Pinch	*(yìk)*	หยิก
Wink	*(krà-phríp-taa)*	กระพริบตา

▶ **Close your eyes.**
(làp-taa)
หลับตา

▶ **Open your eyes.**
(luem-taa)
ลืมตา

▶ **Wave your hand.**
(bòk-mue)
โบกมือ

▶ **Raise your hand.**
(yók-mue)
ยกมือ

Essential Question Words

1. **Who**	*(khrai)*	ใคร
2. **What**	*(à-rai)*	อะไร
3. **Where**	*(thîi-nǎi)*	ที่ไหน
4. **When**	*(mûea-rài)*	เมื่อไร
5. **Why**	*(tham-mai)*	ทำไม
6. **How**	*(yang-ngai)*	ยังไง
7. **Which one?** (referring to an object)	*(an-nǎi)*	อันไหน
8. **Do/Does/ Are/Is...?**	*(mái)*	ไหม
9. **Can...?**	*(dâi-mái)*	ได้ไหม
10. **How much?**	*(thâo-rài)*	เท่าไร

IMPORTANT QUESTIONS

Question 1:

▶ **Where is the _____?**
_____ *(yòu thîi-nǎi)*

_____อยู่ที่ไหน

restaurant	*(ráan-aa-hǎan)*	ร้านอาหาร
market	*(tà-làat)*	ตลาด
bathroom	*(hâwng-nám)*	ห้องน้ำ

Internet café	*(ráan-nèt)*	ร้านเน็ต
pharmacy	*(ráan-khǎay-yaa)*	ร้านขายยา
department store	*(hâang)*	ห้าง
coffee shop	*(ráan-kaa-fae)*	ร้านกาแฟ
bookstore	*(ráan-nǎng-sǔe)*	ร้านหนังสือ
movie theater	*(rong-nǎng)*	โรงหนัง
hotel	*(rong-raem)*	โรงแรม
hospital	*(rong-phá-yaa-baan)*	
	โรงพยาบาล	
bank	*(thá-naa-khaan)*	ธนาคาร
post office	*(prai-sà-nii)*	ไปรษณีย์
police station	*(sà-thǎa-nii-tam-rùat)*	
	สถานีตำรวจ	
school	*(rong-rian)*	โรงเรียน
university	*(má-hǎa-wít-thá-*	มหาวิทยาลัย
	yaa-lai)	

Question 2:

▶ **Are you _____?**
(khun _____ mái)
คุณ _____ ไหม

tired	*(nùeay)*	เหนื่อย
hungry	*(hǐw)*	หิว
thirsty	*(hǐw-nám)*	หิวน้ำ
sick	*(mâi sà-baay)*	ไม่สบาย
happy	*(dii-jai)* *(informal)*	ดีใจ
	(mii-khwaam-sùk) *(formal)*	มีความสุข
angry	*(kròt)*	โกรธ

Question 3:

▶ **Do you have _____?**
(khun mii _____ mái)
คุณมี _____ ไหม

▶ **Do you like _____?**
(khun-châwp _____ mái)
คุณชอบ _____ ไหม

Question 4:

▶ **How much?**

<u>Male</u>	<u>Female</u>
(thâo-rài) (khráp)	*(thâo-rài) (khá)*
เท่าไรครับ	เท่าไรคะ

Question 5:

► **Can you _____?**
(khun _____ dâi-mái)
คุณ _____ ได้ไหม

► **Can I _____?**

<u>Male</u>   <u>Female</u>
(phǒm _____ dâi-mái)   *(chǎn _____ dâi-mái)*
ผม _____ ได้ไหม   ฉัน _____ ได้ไหม

► **Can I hold your hand?**
(jàp-mue dâi-mái)
จับมือได้ไหม

► **Can I hug you?**
(gàwt dâi-mái)
กอดได้ไหม

► **Can I kiss you?**
(jòup dâi-mái)
จูบได้ไหม

Useful Phrases

PHRASE 1:

▶ **I am _____.**

<u>Male</u>	<u>Female</u>
(phŏm) _____	*(chăn)* _____
ผม _____	ฉัน _____

hot	*(ráwn)*	ร้อน
cold	*(năaw)*	หนาว
well	*(sà-baay-dii)*	สบายดี
sick	*(mâi sà-baay)*	ไม่สบาย
lost	*(lŏng-thaang)*	หลงทาง
tired	*(nùeay)*	เหนื่อย
hungry	*(hĭw)*	หิว
thirsty	*(hĭw-nám)*	หิวน้ำ
full	*(ìm)*	อิ่ม
sleepy	*(ngûang-nawn)*	ง่วงนอน
bored	*(bùea)*	เบื่อ
enjoyable/fun	*(sà-nùk)*	สนุก
shy	*(aay)*	อาย
scared	*(klua)*	กลัว
angry	*(kròt)*	โกรธ
stressed	*(khrîat)*	เครียด

excited	*(tùen-tên)*	ตื่นเต้น
happy	*(dii-jai)* [informal]	ดีใจ
	(mii-khwaam-sùk) [formal]	มีความสุข
sad	*(sĭa-jai/sâo)*	เสียใจ/เศร้า
worried	*(klûm-jai)*	กลุ้มใจ
get frightened	*(tòk-jai)*	ตกใจ

PHRASE 2:

▶ **You are _____.**
 (Khun) _____
 คุณ _____

a good person	*(pen-khon-dii)*	เป็นคนดี
funny	*(tà-lòk)*	ตลก
lovely/cute	*(nâa-rák)*	น่ารัก
beautiful	*(sŭay)*	สวย
afraid	*(klua)*	กลัว
naughty	*(son)*	ซน
fat	*(oûan)*	อ้วน
thin, skinny	*(phăwm)*	ผอม
tall	*(sŏung)*	สูง
short (height)	*(tîa)*	เตี้ย
handsome	*(làw)*	หล่อ

skillful, good at	*(kèng)*	เก่ง
smart	*(chà-làat)*	ฉลาด
hardworking	*(khà-yǎn)*	ขยัน
lazy	*(khîi-kìat)*	ขี้เกียจ
shy	*(khîi-aay)*	ขี้อาย
cheerful	*(râa-rerng)*	ร่าเริง
kind, nice	*(jai-dii)*	ใจดี
unkind, mean	*(jai-dam)*	ใจดำ
impatient	*(jai-ráwn)*	ใจร้อน
calm, patient	*(jai-yen)*	ใจเย็น

PHRASE 3:

▶ **I like _____.**

<u>Male</u>	<u>Female</u>
(phǒm-châwp) _____	*(chǎn-châwp)* _____
ผมชอบ _____	ฉันชอบ _____

the beach	*(thá-lay)*	ทะเล
swimming	*(wâay-nám)*	ว่ายน้ำ
movies	*(dou-nǎng)*	ดูหนัง
dining out	*(thaan-aa-hǎan)* [formal]	ทานอาหาร
	(kin aa-hǎan) [informal]	กินอาหาร

walking	*(dern-lên)*	เดินเล่น
Thai boxing	*(muay-thai)*	มวยไทย
river	*(mâe-nám)*	แม่น้ำ
waterfall	*(nám-tòk)*	น้ำตก
mountain	*(phou-khǎo)*	ภูเขา
temple	*(wát)*	วัด
museum	*(phí-phít-thá-phan)*	พิพิธภัณฑ์
run	*(wing)*	วิ่ง
ride a bike	*(khìi-jàk-kà-yaan)*	ขี่จักรยาน
hike	*(dern-pàa)*	เดินป่า
gardening	*(tham-sǔan)*	ทำสวน
dance	*(tên)*	เต้น
listen to music	*(fang-phleng)*	ฟังเพลง
sing	*(ráwng-phleng)*	ร้องเพลง
play musical instruments	*(lên-don-trii)*	เล่นดนตรี
take a trip, travel	*(pai-thîaw)*	ไปเที่ยว

PHRASE 4:

▶ **I do not like _____.**
  Male
  (phŏm mâi-châwp) _____
  ผมไม่ชอบ _____

  Female
  (chăn mâi-châwp) _____
  ฉันไม่ชอบ _____

spicy food	*(aa-hăan-phèt)*	อาหารเผ็ด
smoking	*(sòup-bù-rìi)*	สูบบุหรี่
loud noise	*(sĭang-dang)*	เสียงดัง
lots of people	*(khon-yér)*	คนเยอะ
humid weather	*(aa-kàat-chúen)*	อากาศชื้น
heat	*(aa-kàat-ráwn)*	อากาศร้อน
rain	*(fŏn-tòk)*	ฝนตก
flood	*(nám-thûam)*	น้ำท่วม
mosquito bites	*(yung-kàt)*	ยุงกัด
houseflies	*(má-laeng-wan)*	แมลงวัน
cockroaches	*(má-laeng-sàap)*	แมลงสาบ

PHRASE 5:

▶ **No, thank you.**

Male
(mâi-pen-rai khráp) (khàwp-khun khráp)
ไม่เป็นไรครับ ขอบคุณครับ

Female
(mâi-pen-rai khâ) (khàwp-khun khâ)
ไม่เป็นไรค่ะ ขอบคุณค่ะ

PHRASE 6:

▶ **I would like _____.**

Male	Female
(phǒm khǎw) _____	*(chǎn khǎw)* _____
ผมขอ _____	ฉันขอ _____

PHRASE 7:

▶ **I can _____.**

Male	Female
(phǒm) _____ *(dâi)*	*(chǎn)* _____ *(dâi)*
ผม _____ ได้	ฉัน _____ ได้

PHRASE 8:

▶ **I cannot _____.**

Male	Female
(phǒm _____ *mâi-dâi)*	*(chǎn* _____ *mâi-dâi)*
ผม _____ ไม่ได้	ฉัน _____ ไม่ได้

PART TWO
Everyday Conversations

Introductions

PERSON 1:

▶ **Hello.**

Male	Female
(sà-wàt-dii) (khráp)	*(sà-wàt-dii) (khâ)*
สวัสดีครับ	สวัสดีค่ะ

▶ **How are you?**
(sà-baay-dii mái)
สบายดีไหม

PERSON 2:

▶ **I am fine, thank you, and how are you?**
<u>Male</u>
(sà-baay-dii)(khàwp-khun) (khráp)
(láew khun lâ) (khráp)
สบายดี ขอบคุณรับ แล้วคุณล่ะครับ

Female
(sà-baay-dii)(khàwp-khun) (khâ)
(láew khun lâ) (khá)
สบายดี ขอบคุณค่ะ แล้วคุณล่ะคะ

PERSON 1:

► **My name is _____.**

Male   Female
(phŏm chûe) _____   *(chăn chûe)* _____
ผมชื่อ _____   ฉันชื่อ _____

► **What is your name?**
(khun chûe à-rai)
คุณชื่ออะไร

PERSON 2:

► **My name is _____.**

Male   Female
(phŏm chûe) _____   *(chăn chûe)* _____
ผมชื่อ _____   ฉันชื่อ _____

PERSON 1:

▶ **Nice to meet you.**
   (yin-dii-thîi-dâi-róu-jàk)
   ยินดีที่ได้รู้จัก

PERSON 2:

▶ **Nice to meet you as well!**
   (yin-dii-thîi-dâi-róu-jàk chên-kan)
   ยินดีที่ได้รู้จักเช่นกัน

COMMON GREETINGS

Note: All of these phrases should end with the polite particle *(khráp)* for men, and *(khâ)* for women.

Hello	*(sà-wàt-dii)*	สวัสดี

Note: You can say *(sà-wàt-dii)* สวัสดี to replace "Hi," "Good morning," "Good afternoon," or "Good evening."

Till I see you again.	*(láew-jer-kan)*	แล้วเจอกัน
Good night/	*(făn-dii)*	ฝันดี
have a nice dream.		

Sleep well.	*(làp-sà-baay)*	หลับสบาย
Take care of yourself.	*(dou-lae tua-eng)*	ดูแลตัวเอง
Pardon me.	*(khăw-thôt)*	ขอโทษ
What's up?	*(wâa-ngai)*	ว่าไง
Did you eat yet?	*(kin khâaw rúe-yang)*	กินข้าวหรือยัง

FAMILY RELATIONS

Note: All of these phrases should end with the polite particle *(khráp)* for men, and *(khâ)* for women.

▶ **Do you have a/an _____?**
   (khun-mii) _____
   คุณมี _____

▶ **I have a/an _____.**

Male	Female
(phŏm mii) _____	*(chăn mii)* _____
ผมมี _____	ฉันมี _____

▶ **I do not have a/an _____.**

Male	Female
(phŏm mâi-mii) _____	*(chăn mâi-mii)* _____
ผมไม่มี _____	ฉันไม่มี _____

older brother	*(phîi-chaay)*	พี่ชาย
younger brother	*(náwng-chaay)*	น้องชาย
older sister	*(phîi-sǎaw)*	พี่สาว
younger sister	*(náwng-sǎaw)*	น้องสาว
mother	*(mâe)*	แม่
father	*(phâw)*	พ่อ
daughter	*(lôuk-sǎaw)*	ลูกสาว
son	*(lôuk-chaay)*	ลูกชาย
cousin	*(yâat)*	ญาติ
aunt	*(pâa)*	ป้า
uncle	*(lung)*	ลุง
granddaughter/ niece	*(lǎan-sǎaw)*	หลานสาว
grandson/ nephew	*(lǎan-chaay)*	หลานชาย
niece	*(lǎan-sǎaw)*	หลานสาว
nephew	*(lǎan-chaay)*	หลานชาย
girlfriend/ boyfriend	*(faen)*	แฟน
sweetheart	*(thîi-rák)*	ที่รัก

Getting Around

► **Hello.**

Male	Female
(sà-wàt-dii) (khráp)	*(sà-wàt-dii) (khâ)*
สวัสดีครับ	สวัสดีค่ะ

► **Can you help me please?**
<u>Male</u>
(chûay phǒm dâi-mái)
ช่วยผมได้ไหม

<u>Female</u>
(chûay chǎn dâi-mái)
ช่วยฉันได้ไหม

► **I am lost.**
<u>Male</u>
(phǒm lǒng-thaang)
ผมหลงทาง

<u>Female</u>
(chǎn lǒng-thaang)
ฉันหลงทาง

COMMON PLACES

Note: All of these phrases should end with the polite particle *(khráp)* for men, and *(khâ)* for women.

▶ **Where is _____?**
(_____ yòu thîi-nǎi)
_____ อยู่ที่ไหน

▶ **Do you know the _____?**
(khun róu-jàk _____ mái)
คุณรู้จัก _____ ไหม

▶ **I do not know the _____.**
<u>Male</u>
(phǒm mâi-róu-jàk) _____
ผมไม่รู้จัก _____

<u>Female</u>
(chǎn mâi-róu-jàk) _____
ฉันไม่รู้จัก _____

▶ **How do I get to _____?**
(pai) _____ (yang-ngai)
ไป _____ ยังไง

▶ **Can you take me to _____?**
(pai sòng thîi _____ dâi-mái)
ไปส่งที่ _____ ได้ไหม

restaurant	(ráan-aa-hăan)	ร้านอาหาร
inexpensive but good hotel	(rong-raem tòuk tàe dii)	โรงแรมถูก แต่ดี
bus station	(baw-khăaw-săaw) / (thâa-rót)	บ.ข.ส. / ท่ารถ
the bus	(rót-may)	รถเมล์
Skytrain	(rót-fai-fáa)	รถไฟฟ้า
subway	(rót-fai-tâi-din)	รถไฟใต้ดิน
street	(thà-nŏn)	ถนน
parking lot	(thîi-jàwt-rót)	ที่จอดรถ
garden	(sŭan)	สวน
beach	(thá-lay), (chaay-hàat)	ทะเล, ชายหาด
river	(mâe-nám)	แม่น้ำ
lake	(bueng), (thá-lay-sàap)	บึง, ทะเลสาบ
jungle	(pàa)	ป่า

▶ **Can you take me to the island?**
(pai sòng thîi kàw dâi-mái)
ไปส่งที่เกาะได้ไหม

▶ **Can you take me to the airport?**
(pai sòng thîi sà-nǎam-bin dâi-mái)
ไปส่งที่สนามบินได้ไหม

▶ **Thank you.**

Male	Female
(khàwp-khun khráp)	*(khàwp-khun khâ)*
ขอบคุณครับ	ขอบคุณค่ะ

GETTING DIRECTIONS

Note: All of these phrases should end with the polite particle *(kráp)* for men, and *(khâ)* for women.

▶ **Which way is _____ ?**
(thít) _____ *(yòu thaang-nǎi)*
ทิศ _____ อยู่ทางไหน

▶ **I am going to the _____.**

Male	Female
(phǒm jà pai) _____	*(chǎn jà pai)* _____
ผมจะไป _____	ฉันจะไป _____

north (direction)	*(thít-nǔea)*	ทิศเหนือ
south (direction)	*(thít-tâi)*	ทิศใต้
east (direction)	*(thít-tà-wan-àwk)*	ทิศตะวันออก
west (direction)	*(thít-tà-wan-tòk)*	ทิศตะวันตก

northern (region)	*(pâak-nŭea)*	ภาคเหนือ
southern (region)	*(pâak-tâi)*	ภาคใต้
eastern (region)	*(pâak-tà-wan-àwk)*	ภาคตะวันออก
western (region)	*(pâak-tà-wan-tòk)*	ภาคตะวันตก

▶ **Up**
(khûen)
ขึ้น

▶ **Down**
(long)
ลง

▶ **Make a left turn.**
(líaw-sáay)
เลี้ยวซ้าย

▶ **Make a right turn.**
(líaw-khwăa)
เลี้ยวขวา

▶ **Stop on the on left side.**
(jàwt thaang-sáay)
จอดทางซ้าย

► **Stop on the right side.**
(jàwt thaang-khwǎa)
จอดทางขวา

► **Over here.**
(tîi-nîi)
ที่นี่

► **Over there.**
(tîi-nôn)
ที่โน่น

At the Hotel

► **Hello.**

Male

(sà-wàt-dii) (khráp)
สวัสดีครับ

Female

(sà-wàt-dii) (khâ)
สวัสดีค่ะ

► **Do you have a room available?**
(mii hâwng wâang mái)
มีห้องว่างไหม

► **How much is it per night?**
(khuen lá thâo-rài)
คืนละเท่าไร

▶ **May I rent a room for _____ days?**
(khăw hâwng phák _____ wan)
ขอห้องพัก _____ วัน

▶ **Do you have a restaurant here?**
(thîi-nîi mii ráan-aa-hăan mái)
ที่นี่มีร้านอาหารไหม

In the Taxi

▶ **Hello.**

<u>Male</u>
(sà-wàt-dii) (khráp)
สวัสดีครับ

<u>Female</u>
(sà-wàt-dii) (khâ)
สวัสดีค่ะ

▶ **Do you know the _____?**
(khun róu-jàk _____ mái)
คุณรู้จัก _____ ไหม

▶ **Please go to _____.**

<u>Male</u>
(pai _____ khráp)
ไป _____ ครับ

<u>Female</u>
(pai _____ khâ)
ไป _____ ค่ะ

Note: *pai* is pronounced as a medium length vowel.

▶ _____ **is in the area of** _____.
_____ *(yòu thaew)* _____
_____ อยู่แถว _____

▶ **How much, please?**

Male
(thâo-rài khráp)
เท่าไรครับ

Female
(thâo-rài khá)
เท่าไรคะ

▶ **Thank you.**

Male
(khàwp-khun khráp)
ขอบคุณครับ

Female
(khàwp-khun khâ)
ขอบคุณค่ะ

At the Restaurant

▶ **Hello, I would like _____.**

<u>Male</u>
(sà-wàt-dii khráp) (phǒm khǎw _____)
[more polite]
สวัสดีครับ ผมขอ _____

(sà-wàt-dii khráp) (phǒm aow _____)
[very informal]
สวัสดีครับ ผมเอา _____

<u>Female</u>
(sà-wàt-dii khâ) (chǎn khǎw _____)
[more polite]
สวัสดีค่ะ ฉันขอ _____

(sà-wàt-dii khâ) (chǎn aow _____)
[very informal]
สวัสดีค่ะ ฉันเอา _____

▶ **May I have _____, please?**
(khǎw _____) [more polite]
ขอ _____

▶ **Do you have _____?**
(mii _____ mái)
มี _____ ไหม

▶ **I would like another _____.**
   (khăw _____ iik) [more polite]
   ขอ _____ อีก

   (aow _____ iik) ([very informal]
   เอา _____ อีก

▶ **The food here is delicious!**
   (aa-hăan thîi-nîi aà-ràwy mâak)
   อาหารที่นี่อร่อยมาก

▶ **Please, may I have the bill?**

<u>Male</u>	<u>Female</u>
(Check bin khráp)	*(Check bin khâ)*
เช็คบิลครับ	เช็คบิลค่ะ

▶ **Thank you.**

<u>Male</u>	<u>Female</u>
(khàwp-khun khráp)	*(khàwp-khun khâ)*
ขอบคุณครับ	ขอบคุณค่ะ

FOODS

Pad thai	*(pàt-thai)*	ผัดไทย
Chicken and rice	*(khâaw-man-kài)*	ข้าวมันไก่
Green sweet curry	*(kaeng-khîaw-wăan)*	แกงขียวหวาน

Chicken with cashews	*(kài-pàt-mét-má-mûang)*	ไก่ผัดเม็ดมะม่วง
Spicy shrimp soup	*(tôm-yam-kûng)*	ต้มยำกุ้ง
Sweet/sour chicken	*(pàt-prîaw-wăan-kài)*	ผัดเปรี้ยวหวานไก่
Beef noodle soup	*(kŭay-tĭaw-nûea)*	ก๋วยเตี๋ยวเนื้อ
Chicken noodle soup	*(kŭay-tĭaw-kài)*	ก๋วยเตี๋ยวไก่
Minced pork dish	*(khâaw-pàt-kà-phrao-mŏu)*	ข้าวผัดกะเพราหมู
Fried rice	*(khâaw-pàt)*	ข้าวผัด

BEVERAGES

Water	*(nám)*	น้ำ
Coffee	*(kaa-fae)*	กาแฟ
Orange juice	*(nám-sôm)*	น้ำส้ม
Watermelon shake	*(taeng-mo-pàn)*	แตงโมปั่น
Iced tea	*(chaa-yen)*	ชาเย็น
Hot tea	*(chaa-ráwn)*	ชาร้อน
Lemonade	*(nám-má-naaw)*	น้ำมะนาว
Lemon shake	*(má-naaw-pàn)*	มะนาวปั่น
Fresh milk	*(nom-sòt)*	นมสด

FRUIT

Watermelon	*(taeng-mo)*	แตงโม
Pineapple	*(sàp-pà-rót)*	สับปะรด
Apple	*(áep-pérn)*	แอปเปิ้ล
Orange	*(sôm)*	ส้ม
Mango	*(má-mûang)*	มะม่วง
Banana	*(klûay)*	กล้วย

Shopping

▶ **Hello**

Male	Female
(sà-wàt-dii) (khráp)	*(sà-wàt-dii) (khâ)*
สวัสดีครับ	สวัสดีค่ะ

▶ **How much is this item right here?**
(nîi thâo-rài)
นี่เท่าไร

▶ **Can you give me a small discount?**
(lót dâi-mái)
ลดได้ไหม

▶ **I would like _____ of these.**
(súe _____ an)
ซื้อ _____ อัน

Note: *an* can be changed to other classifiers according to the objects or items.

▶ **If I buy a lot of them, can you give me a discount?**
(súe yér lót dâi-mái)
ซื้อเยอะ ลดได้ไหม

▶ **Do you have a bigger size?**
(mii khà-nàat yài mái)
มีขนาดใหญ่ไหม

▶ **Do you have a smaller size?**
(mii khà-nàat lék mái)
มีขนาดเล็กไหม

▶ **Do you have any other colors?**
(mii sĭi ùen mái)
มีสีอื่นไหม

▶ **Thank you.**

<u>Male</u>	<u>Female</u>
(khàwp-khun khráp)	*(khàwp-khun khâ)*
ขอบคุณครับ	ขอบคุณค่ะ

At the Workplace

ACADEMIC TITLES

Note: All of these phrases should end with the polite particle *(khráp)* for men, and *(khâ)* for women.

President (of a college)	*(à-thí-kaan-baw-dii)*	อธิการบดี
Vice President (of a college)	*(rong-à-thí-kaan-baw-dii)*	รองอธิการบดี

Dean of Faculty	*(khá-ná-baw-dii)*	คณบดี
Deputy Dean	*(rong-khá-ná-baw-dii)*	รองคณบดี
Dr. (Ph.D.)	*(dáwk-têr)*	ด็อกเตอร์
Professor	*(sàat-traa-jaan)*	ศาสตราจารย์
Associate Professor	*(rong-sàat-traa-jaan)*	รองศาสตราจารย์
Assistant Professor	*(phôu-chûay-sàat-traa-jaan)*	ผู้ช่วยศาตราจารย์
Lecturer	*(aa-jaan)*	อาจารย์
Director (of a school)	*(phôu-am-nuay- kaan)*	ผู้อำนวยการ
Deputy Director	*(rong phôu-am-nuay-kaan)*	รองผู้อำนวยการ

▶ **I am a _____.**

<u>Male</u>
(phŏm pen) _____
ผมเป็น _____

<u>Female</u>
(chăn pen) _____
ฉันเป็น _____

▶ **You are _____?**
(khun pcn) _____
คุณเป็น _____

▶ **You are a/an _____, right?**
(khun pen _____ châi-mái)
คุณเป็น _____ ใช่ไหม

PROFESSIONAL AND OTHER JOB TITLES

business person	*(nák-thú-rá-kìt)*	นักธุรกิจ
office worker	*(phá-nák-ngaan)*	พนักงาน
engineer	*(wít-sà-wá-kawn)*	วิศวกร
mechanic	*(châang)*	ช่าง
company worker	*(phá-nák-ngaan) (baw-rí-sàt)*	พนักงานบริษัท
doctor	*(măw)*	หมอ
lawyer	*(thá-naay-khwaam)*	ทนายความ
police officer	*(tam-rùat)*	ตำรวจ
salesperson	*(phá-nák-ngaan khăay)*	พนักงานขาย
worker on a ship	*(lôuk-ruea)*	ลูกเรือ
military person	*(thá-hăan)*	ทหาร
consultant	*(thîi-prùek-săa)*	ที่ปรึกษา
government official	*(khâa-râat-chá-kaan)*	ข้าราชการ

USING THE INTERNET/SMARTPHONE

▶ **Where can I find an Internet café?**
(ráan-in-ter-nèt yóu thîi-nǎi khá/khráp)
ร้านอินเตอร์เน็ตอยู่ที่ไหน คะ/ครับ

▶ **May I _____, please?**
(khǎw _____ khá/khráp)
ขอ _____ คะ/ครับ

get Internet access	*(chái in-ter-nèt)*	ใช้อินเตอร์เน็ต
use the computer	*(chái cawm-phíew-têr)*	ใช้คอมพิวเตอร์
get a Wi-Fi password	*(rá-hàt waay-faay)*	รหัสวายฟาย
get an email address	*(ii-meo)*	อีเมล์

▶ **What is the hourly rate to use the Internet?**
(chái in-ter-nèt chûa-mong thâo-rài khá/khráp)
ใช้อินเตอร์เน็ตชั่วโมงเท่าไร คะ/ครับ

▶ **Do you have _____?**
(khun mii _____ mái)
คุณมี _____ ไหม

Wi-Fi connection	*(waay-faay)*	วายฟาย
computer/laptop	*(cawm-phíew-têr)*	คอมพิวเตอร์
email address	*(ii-meo)*	อีเมล์

► **I cannot** _____

<u>Male</u>
(phŏm _____ mâi-dâi khráp)
ผม _____ ไม่ได้ครับ

<u>Female</u>
(chăn _____ mâi-dâi khâ)
ฉัน _____ ไม่ได้ค่ะ

access to the Internet	*(khâo in-ter-nèt)*	เข้าอินเตอร์เน็ต
connect to Wi-Fi	*(tàw waay-faay)*	ต่อวายฟาย
send an email	*(sòng ii-meo)*	ส่งอีเมล์

PART THREE

Situations, Making Plans, Sightseeing

On the Phone

▶ **Hello.**

Male	Female
(sà-wàt-dii) (khráp)	*(sà-wàt-dii) (khâ)*
สวัสดีครับ	สวัสดีค่ะ

▶ **How are you?**
(sà-baay-dii mái)
สบายดีไหม

▶ **What's up?** [Informal, to use with friends.]
(wâa-ngai)
ว่าไง

▶ **Where are you?**
(khun yòu thîi-nǎi)
คุณอยู่ที่ไหน

▶ **What are you doing?**
(khun tham à-rai)
คุณทำอะไร

▶ **Are you busy?**
(khun wâang mái)
คุณว่างไหม

▶ **I miss you.**
(khít-thǔeng)
คิดถึง

▶ **I want to see you.**

Male

(phǒm yàak jer khun)
ผมอยากเจอคุณ

Female

(chǎn yàak jer khun)
ฉันอยากเจอคุณ

▶ **Do you want to go out to eat?**
(pai kin khâaw mái)
ไปกินข้าวไหม

▶ **Do you want to meet today?**
(wan-níi jer-kan mái)
วันนี้เจอกันไหม

▶ **Meet me at _____.**
(jer-kan thîi) _____
เจอกันที่ _____

Note: It's usually better to suggest a place to meet instead of asking where to meet.

▶ **Meet at what time?**
(jer-kan kìi-mong)
เจอกันกี่โมง

▶ **Okay, see you later.**
(OK) (láew jer-kan)
โอเค แล้วเจอกัน

Emergencies

feel	*(róu-sùek)*	รู้สึก
sick/ill	*(mâi-sà-baay)*	ไม่สบาย
hurt/sore	*(jèp)*	เจ็บ
common cold	*(pen-wàt)*	เป็นหวัด
fever	*(pen-khâi)*	เป็นไข้
headache	*(pùat-hŭa)*	ปวดหัว
toothache	*(pùat-fan)*	ปวดฟัน
stomachache	*(pùat-tháwng)*	ปวดท้อง

backache	*(pùat-lăng)*	ปวดหลัง
sore eyes	*(jèp-taa)*	เจ็บตา
sore throat	*(jèp-khaw)*	เจ็บคอ
cough	*(ai)*	ไอ
vomiting	*(aa-jian)*	อาเจียน
diarrhea	*(tháwng-sĭa)*	ท้องเสีย
skin rash	*(pen-phùen)*	เป็นผื่น
cut/wound	*(phlăe)*	แผล
bleeding	*(lûeat-àwk)*	เลือดออก
food poisoning	*(aa-hăan-*	อาหารเป็นพิษ
	pen-phít)	
dizzy	*(wian-hŭa)*	เวียนหัว
nauseous	*(khlûen-sâi)*	คลื่นไส้
runny nose	*(nám-môuk-lăi)*	น้ำมูกไหล
breathing problem	*(hăay-jai-mâi-àwk)*	หายใจไม่ออก

▶ **I'm feeling dizzy.**
 (chăn/phŏm róu-sùek wian-hŭa)
 ฉัน/ผม รู้สึกเวียนหัว

▶ **I have a headache.**
(chăn/phŏm pùat-hŭa)
ฉัน/ผม   ปวดหัว

▶ **I can't breathe.**
(chăn/phŏm hăay-jai-mâi- àwk)
ฉัน/ผม   หายใจไม่ออก

▶ **Help!**
(chûay-dûay)
ช่วยด้วย

▶ **Can you please help me?**
<u>Male</u>
(chûay phŏm dâi-mái)
ช่วยผมได้ไหม

<u>Female</u>
(chûay chăn dâi-mái)
ช่วยฉันได้ไหม

▶ **I am ill.**

<u>Male</u>	<u>Female</u>
(phŏm mâi sà-baay)	*(chăn mâi sà-baay)*
ผมไม่สบาย	ฉันไม่สบาย

▶ **I need an ambulance.**
(khǎw rót-phá-yaa-baan)
ขอรถพยาบาล

▶ **I need to go to the hospital.**
(pai rong-phá-yaa-baan)
ไปโรงพยาบาล

Note: *pai* is pronounced as a medium length vowel.

▶ **I need my medication.**

Male	Female
(phǒm khǎw yaa)	*(chǎn khǎw yaa)*
ผมขอยา	ฉันขอยา

▶ **I need to call my family.**

Male
(phǒm khǎw tho-hǎa khrâwp-khrua)
ผมขอโทรหาครอบครัว

Female
(chǎn khǎw tho-hǎa khrâwp-khrua)
ฉันขอโทรหาครอบครัว

Counting

ZERO to 10

0	*(sŏun)*	ศูนย์
1	*(nùeng)*	หนึ่ง
2	*(săwng)*	สอง
3	*(săam)*	สาม
4	*(sìi)*	สี่
5	*(hâa)*	ห้า
6	*(hòk)*	หก
7	*(jèt)*	เจ็ด
8	*(pàet)*	แปด
9	*(kâo)*	เก้า
10	*(sìp)*	สิบ

11 to 99

11	*(sìp-èt)*	สิบเอ็ด
12	*(sìp-săwng)*	สิบสอง
20	*(yîi-sìp)*	ยี่สิบ
21	*(yîi-sìp-èt)*	ยี่สิบเอ็ด
22	*(yîi-sìp-săwng)*	ยี่สิบสอง
30	*(săam-sìp)*	สามสิบ

40	*(sìi-sìp)*	สี่สิบ
50	*(hâa-sìp)*	ห้าสิบ
60	*(hòk-sìp)*	หกสิบ
70	*(jèt-sìp)*	เจ็ดสิบ
80	*(pàet-sìp)*	แปดสิบ
90	*(kâo-sìp)*	เก้าสิบ

100 and Higher

100	*(nùeng-róy)*	หนึ่งร้อย
101	*(nùeng-róy-èt)*	หนึ่งร้อยเอ็ด
102	*(nùeng-róy-sǎwng)*	หนึ่งร้อยสอง
200	*(sǎwng-róy)*	สองร้อย
1,000	*(nùeng-phan)*	หนึ่งพัน
1,100	*(nùeng-phan nùeng-róy)*	หนึ่งพัน หนึ่งร้อย
1,101	*(nùeng-phan nùeng-róy-èt)*	หนึ่งพันหนึ่งร้อยเอ็ด
2,000	*(sǎwng-phan)*	สองพัน
10,000	*(nùeng-mùen)*	หนึ่งหมื่น
100,000	*(nùeng-sǎen)*	หนึ่งแสน
1,000,000	*(nùeng-láan)*	หนึ่งล้าน

Money and ATMs

- The currency of Thailand is the baht and the *satang*. One baht is subdivided into 100 *satang*. Banknotes come in denominations of: 20, 50, 100, 500 and 1,000 baht. Coins come in denominations of: 1, 2, 5 and 10 baht, as well as 25 and 50 *satang*.

- The equivalence of US$1 is 30–33 baht depending on foreign currency rate of Thai commercial banks and international commercial banks operating via their branches in Thailand.

- Major credit cards such as Visa, Mastercard, JCB and American Express, are accepted at most hotels, airlines, restaurants and upscale merchants. However, "cash" is still preferred almost everywhere. A number of banks provide a money exchange service, but the rates can vary so you will have to do your own comparisons when in Thailand,

- ATM machines can be found all over Thailand from major cities to small towns. If your bank is a member of banking networks like Cirrus or PLUS, you should not have a problem using your ATM card in Thailand. It is possible that the Thai bank may charge a small fee for using their machine although it is in fact far more likely that you'll be charged by your own bank for using the ATM card in another country.

money, cash	*(ngern)*	เงิน
dollar	*(dawn-lâa)*	ดอลลาร์

baht	*(bàat)*	บาท
bank	*(thá-na-khaan)*	ธนาคาร
exchange money	*(lâek-ngern)*	แลกเงิน
exchange rate	*(àt-traa-lâek-lâek-ngern)*	อัตราแลกเงิน
withdraw	*(thăwn-ngern)*	ถอนเงิน
deposit	*(fàak-ngern)*	ฝากเงิน
transfer money	*(on-ngern)*	โอนเงิน
ATM card	*(bàt-a-thii-em)*	บัตรเอทีเอ็ม
credit card	*(bàt-khre-dìt)*	บัตรเครดิต
ATM machine	*(tôu-a-thii-em)*	ตู้ เอทีเอ็ม
passport	*(năng-sŭe-dern-thaang)*	หนังสือเดินทาง
service fee/ charge	*(khâa-baw-rí-kaan)*	ค่าบริการ

► **Where can I exchange money?**
(lâek-ngern dâi thîi năi)
แลกเงินได้ที่ไหน

► **What time does the bank open?**
(thá-na-khaan pòet kìi-mong)
ธนาคารเปิดกี่โมง

► **What is the exchange rate?**
(àt-traa-lâek-lâek-ngern thâo-rài)
อัตราแลกเงินเท่าไร

► **I'd like to exchange _____ dollars.**
(khăw lâek-ngern _____ dawn-lâa)
ขอแลกเงิน _____ ดอลลาร์

► **Is there an ATM machine around here?**
(mii tôu-a-thii-em mái)
มีตู้เอทีเอ็มไหม

► **What is the fee for using the ATM machine?**
(khâa-baw-rí-kaan a-thii-em thâo-rài)
ค่าบริการเอทีเอ็มเท่าไร

► **Do you accept credit cards?**
(ráp bàt-khre-dìt mái)
รับบัตรเครดิตไหม

Telling Time

HOURS: AFTERNOON

▶ **Noon**

   (thîang-wan)

   เที่ยงวัน

▶ **1 p.m.**

   (bàay-(nùeng)-mong)

   บ่ายโมง

Note that 1 p.m. can be said either *bàay-nùeng-mong* or just *bàay-mong* without using the number one.

▶ **2 p.m.**

   (bàay-sǎwng-mong)

   บ่ายสองโมง

▶ **3 p.m.**

   (bàay-sǎam-mong)

   บ่ายสามโมง

▶ **4 p.m.**

   (sìi-mong-yen)

   สี่โมงเย็น

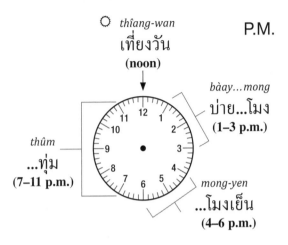

P.M.

thîang-wan
เที่ยงวัน
(noon)

bàay...mong
บ่าย...โมง
(1–3 p.m.)

thûm
...ทุ่ม
(7–11 p.m.)

mong-yen
...โมงเย็น
(4–6 p.m.)

▶ **5 p.m.**
(hâa-mong-yen)
ห้าโมงเย็น

▶ **6 p.m.**
(hòk-mong-yen)
หกโมงเย็น

HOURS: EVENING

▶ **7 p.m.**
(nùeng-thûm)
หนึ่งทุ่ม

▶ **8 p.m.**
   (săwng-thûm)
   สองทุ่ม

▶ **9 p.m.**
   (săam-thûm)
   สามทุ่ม

▶ **10 p.m.**
   (sìi-thûm)
   สี่ทุ่ม

▶ **11 p.m.**
   (hâa-thûm)
   ห้าทุ่ม

▶ **Midnight**
   (thîang-khuen)
   เที่ยงคืน

HOURS: EARLY MORNING

▶ **1 a.m.**
   (tii-nùen)
   ตีหนึ่ง

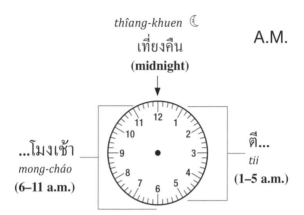

thîang-khuen ☾
เที่ยงคืน
(midnight)

A.M.

...โมงเช้า
mong-cháo
(6–11 a.m.)

ตี...
tii
(1–5 a.m.)

▶ **2 a.m.**
(tii-sǎwng)
ตีสอง

▶ **3 a.m.**
(tii-sǎam)
ตีสาม

▶ **4 a.m.**
(tii-sìi)
ตีสี่

▶ **5 a.m.**
(tii-hâa)
ตีห้า

HOURS: MORNING

► **6 a.m.**
(hòk-mong-cháo)
หกโมงเช้า

► **7 a.m.**
(jèt-mong-cháo)
เจ็ดโมงเช้า

► **8 a.m.**
(pàet-mong-cháo)
แปดโมงเช้า

► **9 a.m.**
(kâo-mong-cháo)
เก้าโมงเช้า

► **10 a.m.**
(sìp-mong-cháo)
สิบโมงเช้า

► **11 a.m.**
(sìp-èt-mong-cháo)
สิบเอ็ดโมงเช้า

▶ **Noon**
  (thîang-wan)
  เที่ยงวัน

MINUTES

Once you know how to tell the time using the hour,
now just add in the minutes using the regular number-
ing system for the Thai language.

Examples:

▶ **1:00 p.m.**
  (bàay-(nùeng)-mong)
  บ่ายโมง

▶ **1:04 p.m.**
  (bàay-(nùeng)-mong) (sìi-naa-thii)
  บ่ายโมงสี่นาที

▶ **1:10 p.m.**
  (bàay-(nùeng)-mong) (sìp-naa-thii)
  บ่ายโมงสิบนาที

▶ **1:15 p.m.**
  (bàay-(nùeng)-mong) (sìp-hâa-naa-thii)
  บ่ายโมงสิบห้านาที

▶ **1:20 p.m.**
(bàay-(nùeng)-mong) (yîi-sìp-naa-thii)
บ่ายโมงยี่สิบนาที

▶ **1:30 p.m.**
(bàay-(nùeng)-mong) (sǎam-sìp-naa-thii) /
(bàay-(nùeng)-mong) (krûeng)
บ่ายโมงสามสิบนาที / บ่ายโมงครึ่ง

▶ **1:45 p.m.**
(bàay-(nùeng)-mong) (sìi-sìp-hâa-naa-thii)
บ่ายโมงสี่สิบห้านาที

TIMES OF THE DAY

Note: All of these phrases should end with the polite particle *(khráp)* for men, and *(khâ)* for women.

▶ **Let's meet in the _____.**
(jer-kan) _____
เจอกัน _____

▶ **I am busy.**

<u>Male</u>   <u>Female</u>
(phǒm mâi-wâang)   *(chǎn mâi-wâang)*
ผมไม่ว่าง   ฉันไม่ว่าง

▶ **Are you available in the _____?**
_____ *(khun wâang mái)*
_____ คุณว่างไหม

morning	*(tawn-cháo)*	ตอนเช้า
daytime	*(klaang-wan)*	กลางวัน
night	*(tawn-khâm)*	ตอนค่ำ
afternoon	*(tawn-bàay)*	ตอนบ่าย
evening	*(tawn-yen)*	ตอนเย็น
late evening	*(tawn-hǔa-khâm)*	ตอนหัวค่ำ
early morning	*(cháo-tru)*	เช้าตรู่

Days of the Week

Monday	*(wan-jan)*	วันจันทร์
Tuesday	*(wan-ang-khaan)*	วันอังคาร
Wednesday	*(wan-phút)*	วันพุธ
Thursday	*(wan-phá-rúe-hàt)*	วันพฤหัสฯ
Friday	*(wan-sùk)*	วันศุกร์
Saturday	*(wan-săo)*	วันเสาร์
Sunday	*(wan-aa-thít)*	วันอาทิตย์

Months of the Year

January	*(mók-kà-raa-khom)*	มกราคม
February	*(kum-phaa-phan)*	กุมภาพันธ์
March	*(mii-naa-kom)*	มีนาคม
April	*(may-săa-yon)*	เมษายน
May	*(phrúet-sà-phaa-khom)*	พฤษภาคม
June	*(mí-thù-naa-yon)*	มิถุนายน
July	*(kà-rá-kà-daa-khom)*	กรกฎาคม
August	*(sĭng-hăa-khom)*	สิงหาคม
September	*(kan-yaa-yon)*	กันยายน
October	*(tù-laa-khom)*	ตุลาคม
November	*(phrúet-sà-jì-kaa-yon)*	พฤศจิกายน
December	*(than-waa-khom)*	ธันวาคม

Common Objects

Note: All of these phrases should end with the polite
particle *(khráp)* for men, and *(khâ)* for women.

▶ **I'm looking for _____.**
Male
(phǒm yàak-dâi) _____
ผมอยากได้ _____

Female
(chǎn yàak-dâi) _____
ฉันอยากได้ _____

▶ **Do you have _____?**
(khun mii) _____ *(mái)*
คุณมี _____ ไหม

▶ **Can I have (a/an) _____ ?**
(khǎw) _____
ขอ _____

pen	*(pàak-kaa)*	ปากกา
pencil	*(din-sǎw)*	ดินสอ
(some) paper	*(krá-dàat)*	กระดาษ
glass	*(kâew)*	แก้ว
chair	*(kâo-îi)*	เก้าอี้

table	*(tó)*	โต๊ะ
plate	*(jaan)*	จาน
fork	*(sâwm)*	ส้อม
spoon	*(cháwn)*	ช้อน
chopsticks	*(tà-kìap)*	ตะเกียบ
knife	*(mîit)*	มีด
hairbrush/comb	*(wǐi)*	หวี
mobile phone (cell phone)	*(tho-rá-sàp-mue-thǔe)*	โทรศัพท์มือถือ
car	*(rót-yon)*	รถยนต์
shirt	*(sûea)*	เสื้อ
pants	*(kaang-keng)*	กางเกง
shorts	*(kaang-keng-khǎa-sán)*	กางเกงขาสั้น
shoes	*(rawng-tháo)*	รองเท้า
socks	*(thǔng-tháo)*	ถุงเท้า
watch	*(naa-lí-kaa)*	นาฬิกา
glasses	*(wâen-taa)*	แว่นตา
sunglasses	*(wâen-gan-dàet)*	แว่นกันแดด
toothbrush	*(praeng-sǐi-fan)*	แปรงสีฟัน
toothpaste	*(yaa-sǐi-fan)*	ยาสีฟัน
soap	*(sà-bòu)*	สบู่
shampoo	*(yaa-sà-phǒm)*	ยาสระผม

bed	*(tiang)*	เตียง
blanket	*(phâa-hòm)*	ผ้าห่ม
pillow	*(mǎwn)*	หมอน
window	*(nâa-tàang)*	หน้าต่าง
mirror	*(krà-jòk)*	กระจก
door	*(prà-tou)*	ประตู

Air Travel

Traveling by plane in Thailand is generally convenient and inexpensive. There are several main airlines with extensive domestic routes—Thai Airways, Thai Smile, Bangkok Airways, Nok Air and Air Asia. Thailand has a number of airports that service both domestic and international air traffic, as well as many more that only serve domestic flights.

There are two main airports in Bangkok. Suvarnab-humi Airport is the premier Thailand airport and serves as a hub for international transit passengers as well as a gateway to various Thai destinations. On the other hand, Don Mueang International Airport has been re-opened and has become a regional commuter flight hub and the low-cost airlines hub since 2012.

airport	*(sà-năam-bin)*	สนามบิน
airplane	*(krûeang-bin)*	เครื่องบิน
airline	*(săay-kaan-bin)*	สายการบิน
reserve	*(jawng)*	จอง
ticket	*(tŭa)*	ตั๋ว
fare	*(khâa-tŭa)*	ค่าตั๋ว
one way	*(thîaw-diaw)*	เที่ยวเดียว
round trip	*(pai-klàp)*	ไปกลับ
available	*(wâang)*	ว่าง
flight	*(thîaw-bin)*	เที่ยวบิน
seat	*(thîi-nâng)*	ที่นั่ง
aisle	*(thaang-dern)*	ทางเดิน
window	*(nâa-tàang)*	หน้าต่าง
board	*(khûen)*	ขึ้น
arrive	*(thŭeng)*	ถึง
depart	*(àwk)*	ออก
gate	*(prà-tou)*	ประตู

luggage/ baggage	*(krà-păo)*	กระเป๋า
left luggage	*(fàak-krà-păo)*	ฝากกระเป๋า
direct flight	*(thîaw-bin-trong)*	เที่ยวบินตรง
passport	*(năng-sŭe-doen-thaang)*	หนังสือเดินทาง
passenger	*(phôu-doy-săan)*	ผู้โดยสาร
first class	*(chán-nùeng)*	ชั้นหนึ่ง
business class	*(chán-thú-rá-kìt)*	ชั้นธุรกิจ
economy class	*(chán-prà-yàt)*	ชั้นประหยัด
domestic	*(nai-prà-thêt)*	ในประเทศ
international	*(tàang-prà-thêt)*	ต่างประเทศ

► **I'd like to reserve two seats to _____.**
(khăw jawng tŭa pai _____ săwng thîi-nâng)
ขอจองตั๋วไป _____ สองที่นั่ง

► **How much is a one-way ticket?**
(khâa-tŭa thîaw-diaw thâo-rài)
ค่าตั๋วเที่ยวเดียวเท่าไร

► **How much is a round-trip ticket?**
(khâa-tŭa pai-klàp thâo-rài)
ค่าตั๋วไปกลับเท่าไร

► **Can I get an aisle seat, please?**
(khăw thîi-nâng rim thaang-dern)
ขอที่นั่งริมทางเดิน

► **Can I get a window seat?**
(khăw thîi-nâng rim nâa-tàang)
ขอที่นั่งริมหน้าต่าง

► **What is the departure time?**
(krûeang-bin àwk kìi-mong)
เครื่องบินออกกี่โมง

► **What is the arrival time?**
(krûeang-bin thŭeng kìi-mong)
เครื่องบินถึงกี่โมง

► **How long is the flight to _____?**
(krûeang-bin pai _____ kìi-chûa-mong)
เครื่องบินไป _____ กี่ชั่วโมง

► **Is it a direct flight, or do I have to change planes?**
(thîaw-bin-trong rŭe tâwng plìan krûeang-bin)
เที่ยวบินตรงหรือต้องเปลี่ยนเครื่องบิน

▶ **What is the boarding gate?**
(khûen krûeang-bin prà-tou à-rai)
ขึ้นเครื่องบินประตูอะไร

▶ **May I leave my luggage?**
(fàak-krà-pǎo dâi-mái)
ฝากกระเป๋าได้ไหม

Modes of Transport in Towns and Cities

Getting around in Thailand is easy and inexpensive. If you are traveling in Bangkok, then taking a **taxi** can be a convenient and affordable way to get around. Most taxis in Thailand run on meters now, but it's still a good idea to check if the taxi has a running meter before you get in.

Tuk tuks and **motorbike taxis** are also available in Bangkok and large cities. They cost less than typical taxis, but are considerably less safe. If you decide to use either of these modes of transportation, make sure that you negotiate a price in advance.

Skytrain and subway, commonly known as the **BTS** and **MRT**, respectively, can be another option to alleviate the capital city's notorious traffic jams.

For travel within large provincial cities, public transport is typically supplied by *sŏng-thăew* (**two-row mini-bus**). Its name is from the two benches of seats fixed along either side of the back of the truck. Additionally a roof is fitted over the rear of the vehicle, to which curtains and plastic sheeting to keep out rain may be attached. *Song-thaew* are used both within towns and cities and for longer routes between towns and villages.

take someone to	*(phaa-pai)*	พาไป
taxi	*(táek-sîi)*	แท็กซี่
motorbike taxis	*(win-maw-ter-sai)*	วินมอเตอร์ไซค์
metro bus	*(rót-may)*	รถเมล์
bus stop	*(pâay-rót-may)*	ป้ายรถเมล์
skytrain (BTS)	*(rót-fai-fáa)*	รถไฟฟ้า

subway (MRT)	*(rót-fai-tâi-din)*	รถไฟใต้ดิน
two-row minibus	*(rót-sŏng-thăew)*	รถสองแถว
number/ route/line	*(săay)*	สาย
fare	*(khâa-tŭa)*	ค่าตั๋ว
get on/take a transport	*(khûen)*	ขึ้น
get off/alight	*(long)*	ลง

▶ **I need a taxi, please.**
(khăw táek-sîi khâ/khráp)
ขอแท็กซี่ ค่ะ/ครับ

▶ **I'd like to go to _____, please.**
(pai _____ khâ/khráp)
ไป _____ ค่ะ/ครับ

▶ **Is your meter on?**
(pèrt mí-têr mái)
เปิดมิเตอร์ไหม

▶ **Could you take me to _____, please?**
(chûay phaa-pai thîi _____)
ช่วยพาไปที่ _____

▶ **How much is it to go to _____?**
   (pai _____ thâo-rài)
   ไป _____ เท่าไร

▶ **Which number/line does it go to _____?**
   (khûen sǎay nǎi pai _____)
   ขึ้นสายไหนไป _____

▶ **Does this bus/minibus pass _____?**
   (rót sǎay níi phàan _____ mái)
   รถสายนี้ผ่าน _____ ไหม

▶ **I'd like to get off at _____.**
   (khǎw long thîi _____)
   ขอลงที่ _____

TRAVELING BY BUS AND TRAIN

For long distance travel, the **train** is generally the best option. Although train travel is the slowest way to get from one place to another, it is by far the safest and most convenient for the price. Thai trains are separated into three different classes. First- and second-class cars typically have comfortable seats and air conditioning, including decent sleeper units for overnight trips. Third-class cars are fan cooled and seats are either padded or hard wood.

Buses are also another option for the most convenient way of getting around the country. Thailand is connected by an excellent bus/coach system. The buses themselves vary in levels of comfort and service. Non air-con buses are the cheapest and slowest. These buses stop in every little town and pick up passengers at any point along the route. Air-con buses are faster, more comfortable, and very reasonably priced. There are also VIP buses providing more leg room for each passenger for long-distance journeys.

train	(rót-fai)	รถไฟ
train station	(sà-thăa-nii rót-fai)	สถานีรถไฟ
bogie	(tôu)	ตู้
passenger car	(tôu-nâng)	ตู้นั่ง
sleeping car	(tôu-nawn)	ตู้นอน
dining car	(tôu-sà-biang)	ตู้เสบียง
ordinary train	(rót-tham-má-daa)	รถธรรมดา
rapid train	(rót-rew)	รถเร็ว
express train	(rót-dùan)	รถด่วน
special express train	(rót-dùan-phí-sèt)	รถด่วนพิเศษ
first class	(chán-nùeng)	ชั้นหนึ่ง
second class	(chán-săwng)	ชั้นสอง
third class	(chán-săam)	ชั้นสาม

platform/terminal	*(chaan-chaa-laa)*	ชานชาลา
non air-con bus	*(rót-doi-san-mai-prap-akat),* *(rót-phat-lom)*	รถโดยสารไม่ปรับอากาศ, รถพัดลม
air-con bus/coach	*(rót-thua)*	รถทัวร์
bus station (city)	*(sà-thăa-nii...)*	สถานี...
bus station (local)	*(baw-khăaw-săaw/ thâa-rót)*	บ.ข.ส./ท่ารถ
air conditioning (A/C)	*(ae)*	แอร์
vehicle	*(rót)*	รถ
car	*(rót-kěng)*	รถเก๋ง
van	*(rót-tôu)*	รถตู้
get on	*(khûen)*	ขึ้น
get off	*(long)*	ลง
buy	*(súe)*	ซื้อ
ticket	*(tŭa)*	ตั๋ว
ticket office	*(hâwng-khăay-tŭa)*	ห้องขายตั๋ว
fare	*(khâa-tŭa)*	ค่าตั๋ว
single (ticket)	*(thîaw-diaw)*	เที่ยวเดียว
return (ticket)	*(pai-klàp)*	ไปกลับ
leave/depart	*(àwk)*	ออก
arrive	*(thŭeng)*	ถึง
stop	*(jàwt)*	จอด
sit	*(nâng)*	นั่ง

▶ **Where is the ticket office?**
(hâwng-khǎay-tǔa yòu thîi-nǎi)
ห้องขายตั๋วอยู่ที่ไหน

▶ **May I buy a ticket to _____?**
(khǎw súe tǔa pai _____)
ขอซื้อตั๋วไป _____

▶ **When is there a bus/train to _____?**
(mii rót-thua/rót-fai pai _____ kìi-mong)
มี รถทัวร์/รถไฟ ไป _____ กี่โมง

▶ **How much is a single/return ticket?**
(khâa-tǔa thîaw-diaw/pai-klàp thâo-rài)
ค่าตั๋ว เที่ยวเดียว/ไปกลับ เท่าไร

▶ **How much is a first class/second class train?**
(khâa-tǔa chán-nùeng/chán-sǎwng thâo-rài)
ค่าตั๋ว ชั้นหนึ่ง/ชั้นสอง เท่าไร

▶ **What time does the bus/train leave?**
(rót-thua/rót-fai àwk kìi-mong)
รถทัวร์/รถไฟ ออกกี่โมง

▶ **What time does the bus/train arrive?**
(rót-thua/rót-fai thŭeng kìi-mong)
รถทัวร์/รถไฟ ถึงกี่โมง

▶ **How many hours is it to _____?**
(pai _____ kìi-chûa-mong)
ไป _____ กี่ชั่วโมง

▶ **Are there express trains to _____ today?**
(wan-níi mii rót-dùan pai _____ mái)
วันนี้มีรถด่วนไป _____ ไหม

▶ **Are there sleeping cars on second-class trains?**
(chán-săwng mii tôu-nawn mái)
ชั้นสองมีตู้นอนไหม

▶ **Which platform/terminal can I get on the bus/train?**
(khûen rót thîi chaan-chaa-laa năi)
ขึ้นรถที่ชานชาลาไหน

▶ **Do you mind if I sit here?**
(nâng thîi-nîi dâi-mái)
นั่งที่นี่ได้ไหม

▶ **Does this train/bus stop at _____?**
(rót jàwt thîi _____ mái)
รถจอดที่ _____ ไหม

▶ **Could you please stop at _____?**
(jàwt thîi _____ dûay)
จอดที่ _____ ได้ไหม

▶ **Could you tell me when we get to _____,
please?**
(chûay bàwk dûay thâa thŭeng _____)
ช่วยบอกด้วยถ้าถึง _____

The Weather

Note: All of these phrases should end with the polite particle *(khráp)* for men, and *(khâ)* for women.

▶ **What's the weather like today?**
(wan-níi aa-kàat pen yang-ngai)
วันนี้อากาศเป็นยังไง

▶ **It's _____ today.**
(wan-níi) _____
วันนี้ _____

▶ **It is _____ today?**
(wan-níi _____ mái)
วันนี้ _____ ไหม

hot	*(ráwn)*	ร้อน
cool	*(yen)*	เย็น
cold	*(năaw)*	เย็น

▶ **I am cold.**

<u>Male</u>	<u>Female</u>
(phŏm năaw)	*(chăn năaw)*
ผมหนาว	ฉันหนาว

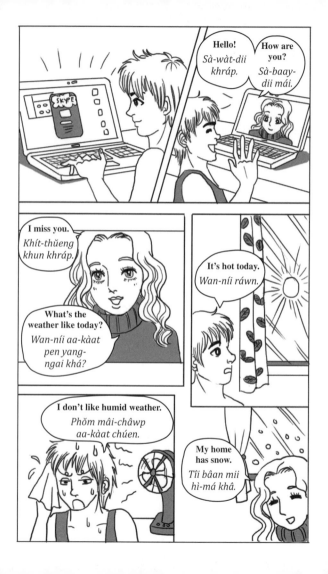

rainy	*(fǒn-tòk)*	ฝนตก
humid	*(chúen)*	ชื้น
ice	*(nám-khàeng)*	น้ำแข็ง
windy	*(lom-raeng)*	ลมแรง
sunny	*(dàet-raeng)*	แดดแรง
bright	*(sà-wàang)*	สว่าง
cloudy	*(mii-mêk)*	มีเมฆ
warm	*(òp-ùn)*	อบอุ่น
mild (just right)	*(phaw-dii)*	พอดี
good (pleasant)	*(dii)*	ดี
beautiful	*(sǔay)*	สวย

▶ **The streets are wet.**
  (thà-nǒn pìak)
  ถนนเปียก

▶ **My home has snow.**
  (tîi bâan mii hì-má)
  ที่บ้านมี หิมะ

PART FOUR

Exploring Thailand

Public Holidays and Festivals

PUBLIC HOLIDAYS

When traveling to Thailand, it's important to know the major national holidays celebrated throughout the country. Some holidays in Thailand follow the Western calendar, and occur on the same date each year. Most Buddhist holidays on the Thai calendar are based on the lunar calendar and therefore will occur on different days from year to year. If the date of a holiday or festival falls on a weekend, the next working day will be taken as a holiday. Here is a list of the most important public holidays in Thailand.

New Year's Day (Jan 01)	*(wan pii-mài)*	วันปีใหม่
Makha Bucha (3rd Thai lunar month)	*(wan maa-khá-bou-chaa)*	วันมาฆบูชา
Chakri Memorial Day (April 06)	*(wan jàk-krii)*	วันจักรี

Songkran/Thai New Year (April 13-15)	*(wan song-kraan)*	วันสงกรานต์
Labour Day (May 01)	*(wan raeng-ngaan)*	วันแรงงาน
Coronation Day (May 05)	*(wan chat-trà-mong-khon)*	วันฉัตรมงคล
Royal Ploughing Ceremony/ Farmer's Day (May, arbitrary date)	*(wan phûet-mong-khon)*	วันพืชมงคล
Visakha Bucha Day (6th Thai lunar month)	*(wan wí-sǎa-khà-bou-chaa)*	วันวิสาขบูชา
Asanha Bucha (8th Thai lunar month)	*(wan aa-sǎan-hà-bou-chaa)*	วันอาสาฬหบูชา
Beginning of Vassa (8th Thai lunar month)	*(wan khâo-phan-sǎa)*	วันเข้าพรรษา
The Queen's Birthday/ National Mother's Day (Aug 12)	*(wan cha-lǒem-phrá-chon-má-phan-sǎa phrá-baw-rom-má-raa-chí-nii-nâat/ wan mâe-hàeng-châat)*	วันแม่แห่งชาติ

Chulalongkorn Day (Oct 23)	*(wan pì-yá-má-hǎa-râat)*	วันปิยมหาราช
The King's Birthday/ National Father's Day (Dec 5)	*(wan cha-lǒem-phrá-chon-má-phan-sǎa phrá-jâo-yòu-hǔa/wan-phâw-hàeng-châat)*	วันพ่อแห่งชาติ
Constitution Day (Dec 10)	*(wan rát-thá-tham-má-noun)*	วันรัฐธรรมนูญ
New Year's Eve (Dec 31)	*(wan sîn-pii)*	วันสิ้นปี

There are also numerous regional and local festivals in addition to the holidays.

THAI FESTIVALS

Chinese New Year

Since Thai people have a strong Chinese heritage, Chinese traditions like the Lunar New Year *(Wan Trùt Jiin)* have become an integral part of Thai culture. So Chinese New Year is observed for several days and nights all across Thailand. Homes and businesses are cleaned thoroughly from top to bottom and then the brooms are put away until after the festival, as tradition dictates that otherwise good luck may be swept away. On the last day of the "old" year, people begin to offer prayers to the Gods and to their ancestors. Even more prayers are offered the next day which is the first day of the New Year.

Chinese New Year celebrations in Bangkok

Songkran is celebrated with much splashing of water nowadays.

Songkran is celebrated in Thailand as the traditional New Year's Day from 13 to 15 April. The first day of the Songkran period is an important day to make good deeds. People visit temples to listen to the Dharma. Also they give alms to monks. Traditionally, the festival is about cleaning, purification, and fresh starts. Houses are cleaned, Buddha statues are gently washed with scented water, and elders are honored by pouring water respectfully over their hands. While pouring the water in this manner, people say good wishes and words of blessing for the coming New Year. But nowadays the Songkran festival is better known for its splashing water madness.

Loy Krathong

This festival is held on the night of the twelfth full moon. Although not a national holiday, this is an important festival. Several translations of *krathong* are found, such as "floating crown," "floating boat," "floating decoration." A *krathong* is decorated with elaborately-folded banana leaves, incense sticks, and a candle. A small coin is sometimes included as an offering to the river spirits. Thais launch their *krathong* on a river, canal or a pond, making a wish as they do so. The festival may originate from an ancient ritual of paying respect to the water spirits.

Chinese Vegetarian Festival

It is on the ninth Chinese lunar month (September–October) and is celebrated throughout the entire country. During a period of nine days, those who are participating in the festival dress all in white and *gin jay* (กินเจ), which has come to be translated as abstinence from eating meat, poultry, seafood, and dairy products. Vendors and proprietors of restaurants indicate that *jay* food is for sale at their establishments by putting a yellow flag out with the word เจ *(jay)* written on it in red.

Pavarana

It is a Buddhist holy day celebrated on the full moon of the eleventh lunar month. It marks the end of the month of **Vassa**, sometimes called "the end of Buddhist Lent." This is a day when many Thai people will visit a temple, often their local temple in their birthplace, to pray and to bring offerings. The most famous event on this day is the **Naga Fireballs** or *Bâng Fai Phá-yaa-nâak* (บั้งไฟพญานาค), in which glowing egg-sized balls rise out of the Mekong River, around the town of Nong Khai.

Popular Tourist Destinations

BANGKOK (กรุงเทพ)

Pronounced: *krung-thêp*

Grand Palace (พระบรมมหาราชวัง)
Pronounced: *(Phrá Baw-rom Má-hǎa Râat-chá-wang)*

Built in 1782 and home of the Thai King and the Royal court, the Grand Palace is a must-see that no visit to Bangkok would be complete without. It is undoubtedly the city's most famous landmark. ·

Wat Phra Kaew (วัดพระแก้ว) (Temple of the Emerald Buddha)—It contains the beautiful Emerald Buddha that dates back to the 14th century.

Wat Pho (วัดโพธิ์) (Temple of the Reclining Buddha)
Located behind the Emerald Buddha. It is one of the largest temples in Thailand and is famous for its large reclining Buddha measuring 49 meters long.

Wat Arun (วัดอรุณ) (Temple of the Dawn)—This temple is on the bank of the Chao Phraya River and is one of Bangkok's world-famous landmarks. It has an amazing steeple that is over 72 meters high and decorated with tiny pieces of colored glass and Chinese porcelain arranged into intricate patterns. At night the temple is lit, which makes for one of the best photos of your trip.

Chatuchak Market (ตลาดจตุจักร)
Pronounced: *(tà-làat jà-tù-jàk)*—One of the world's
largest wholesale weekend markets covering an area
of about 35 acres, it has more than 9,000 booths sell-
ing goods from every part of Thailand. Many vendors
come from local factories so you can find some great
deals here. If you are looking for something in particular in Thailand, Chatuchak is the place to go! This is a
must-visit when you are looking for interesting gifts to
bring back as souvenirs. One thing to keep in mind: it
is very hot there in the summer months.

MBK also known as *(Mah boon krong)* (มาบุญครอง)
This is another must-visit place if you are a shopper!
MBK is probably Bangkok's most legendary shopping mall, with its eight floors packed with over 2,500
shops. You can find everything in MBK from cloth-
ing, fashion accessories, handbags, leather products
and luggage to furniture, mobile phones and high-end
electronics. Also you can find knockoff designer items
in the smaller shops on the top floors!

KANCHANABURI (กาญจนบุรี**)**

Pronounced: *(kaan-jà-ná-bù-rii)*—Kanchanaburi
is home to the famous bridge over the River Kwai.
During World War II, Japan constructed a railroad
from Thailand to Burma. The railway over the bridge
winds through the rocky Three Pagodas Pass for about

A train passes on the famous bridge over the River Kwai.

300 miles. This is now known as the Death Railway because prisoners-of-war supplied the workforce to build the railway, and due to the difficult terrain, thousands of laborers lost their lives. It is believed that one life was lost for each railroad tie laid in the track. You can take the train from the Bangkok train station and stop to see the Bridge on your way to Chiang Mai.

CHIANG MAI (เชียงใหม่)

Pronounced: *(Chiang-mài)*

Chiang Mai is in the north of Thailand in the mountainous region of the country.

Night train to Chiang Mai from Bangkok (รถไฟ
ตอนเย็นจะไปเชียงใหม่)—A very interesting way to
get to Chang Mai and see some of the hidden parts of
Thailand is to take the train. There are several evening
trains leaving from the Bangkok train station going the
scenic route to Chiang Mai. The first train leaves
Bangkok at 6 p.m. and arrives in Chiang Mai around
7 p.m. After dinner your train seats can be converted
into bunk beds for a comfortable rest before you arrive
in Chiang Mai in the morning.

Night Market and Bazaar (ตลาดนัดกลางคืน)
Pronounced: *(tà-làat nat klāngkheūn)*—This is a fun
place to visit after dinner and into the evening. Walking
around and looking at all the local handicrafts may take
you longer than you planned. Every evening, the center
of Chiang Mai comes alive with the massive night
market that stretches for several blocks and includes
restaurants, bars and entertainment. Dinner and souvenir
shopping make for a full evening of enjoyment in this
area.

Wat Phrathat Doi Suthep (วัดพระธาตุดอยสุเทพ)—
This impressive temple is located at the top of a huge
mountain about 15 km from the city of Chiang Mai.
There is a massive 300-step Naga snake staircase lead-
ing up to the temple. There is also a cable car that goes
to the top if you prefer not to walk the steps. From the
top you will have an amazing view of Chiang Mai and

Feasting on local fare in Chiang Mai's night market

the landscape. The ride up the swirly mountain road makes for an interesting day trip in itself.

Muang On Cave (ถ้ำเมืองออน)—For something different, make a trip to visit Muang On Cave. The cave
is located about 35 km outside the city of Chiang Mai
in the San Kamphaeng District. From the car park you
have to climb up the 180-step Naga snake staircase to
the cave entrance. Be sure to bring water or buy drinks
from the local vendors in the car park below the cave
entrance. At the cave entrance you can hire a local
guide to walk you through the cave.

Once inside you will find there are two steep stair-
cases descending down to the main cave. The cave is
lit with a few fluorescent lights ample enough to see,
but I recommend renting a flashlight from the guide.
When you reach the first platform deck look to the left
and you will see what the Thai say is a huge fossilized
dinosaur skeleton. When you reach the main cavern
floor you will see a 30-foot-long reclining Buddha.

After you have finished exploring the caverns, and
if you are feeling strong, there are two interesting small
temples at the top of the cave. But be prepared for the
long climb up the winding path of 709 more steps from
the cave entrance.

A visit to Muang On Cave is a great day trip espe-
cially if combined with a visit to the hot springs just
outside the city of San Kamphaeng (สันกำแพง) where
you can soak in the wonderful sulfur baths to ease your
aches from all the step climbing.

Hot springs in the city of San Kampheang, Chiang Mai

Hot springs in San Kamphaeng (สันกำแพง)—The hot springs are located about 40 km outside of Chiang Mai or just 3 km down the road from the Muang On Cave. There are several hot springs in the same area, both public and private. Inside the park, there is a coed swimming pool filled with hot sulfur water. There are many local vendors to buy a swimsuit or sandals from if you forgot to pack them. There is also a small cement creek running through the length of the park if you just want to dip your feet or legs in the sulfur bath. Inside the Hot Springs Park there are cottages for rent if you want to spend the evening.

Elephant Trekking (ขี่ช้าง)
Pronounced: *(kìi-cháang)*—This can be a full day adventure and an awesome chance to take pictures. You can book a tour at any local travel agency for an affordable price.

Chiang Mai Flower Festival—In early February every year, the city of Chiang Mai comes alive with an amazing display of flowers. There is a beauty contest and a flower parade with highly decorated floats that travel though the central part of the city. Main streets are closed off for the parade and to make room for the many street vendors.

Elephant trekking is popular with tourists.

PHUKET (ภูเก็ต)

Phuket is home to some of the world's most amazing beaches. From blue lagoons to tangerine sunsets, Phuket has it all. Along with the usual assortment of water sports such as diving, snorkeling and wind surfing, Phuket also offers a few less common activities. For the more adventurous: try sea kayaking though caves or a guided cave tour.

Koh Phi Phi (เกาะพีพี)

Pronounced: *(Kàw Phii-Phii)*—Phi Phi Island is Thailand's island rock star. If you have ever seen a movie with an amazing island-like landscape, chances are good that it is Koh Phi Phi. Even with all the hype, it still lives up to its reputation for beauty and allure. Koh Phi Phi is extremely beautiful and laid back but one of the more expensive places to visit in Thailand.

Krabi (กระบี่)—This is another area with beautiful pristine white sandy beaches. The towering limestone cliffs and crevasses make the coastline of Krabi breathtaking. When you sit on a beach in Krabi, it is like sitting inside a picture on a postcard. World class rock climbing can be found at Railay Beach (อ่าวไร่เลย์) with its interesting rock formations that resemble a sort of coastal Jurassic Park.

An aerial view of Phuket

PATTAYA (พัทยา)

Pronounced: *(Phát-thá-yaa)*—Pattaya is a tourist city two hours south of Bangkok and is the closest beach town. It is sometimes referred to as "Las Vegas on steroids" because of its reputation for nightlife. Pattaya is filled with a wide assortment of evening activities ranging from sea food restaurants to strip clubs, from live music to go-carting.

New Year's celebrations in Pattaya

Pattaya New Year's Eve Countdown—If you like fireworks on New Year's Eve then this is the place for you if you do not mind crowds. You can watch an amazing 200-degree panoramic firework display.

Pattaya International Music Festival—This festival is usually held in the second week of March. Top Asian performers and international acts perform on a daily schedule.

HUA HIN (หัวหิน)
Pronounced: *(Hŭa-hĭn)*

Hua Hin is a famous beach resort town some 200 km south of Bangkok. Hua Hin is closely associated with the Thai royalty and therefore more of an upscale tourist destination. The beaches are clean; the water is clear and the atmosphere is relaxed.

A shopping mall in Hua Hin

RAYONG (ระยอง)

Pronounced: *(Rá-yawng)*

Rayong is a quiet fishing town about 200 km south of Bangkok. If you are a fresh fruit lover then Rayong is the place to visit. Most of the exotic delicious fruits—durian, mangosteen, lichee, mango and dragonfruit, to name a few—all hail from Rayong.

Koh Samet-Rayong (เกาะเสม็ด)

Pronounced: *(Kàw Sà-mèt)*—This is the closest island to Bangkok and is conveniently just a short drive away.

A great place for relaxation, Koh Samet-Rayong is popular with tourists and locals alike.

Koh Chang-Rayong (เกาะช้าง)

Pronounced: *(Kàw Cháang)*—This is the central point of Koh Chang National Marine Park, part of a marine national park consisting of mostly uninhabited islands. The monkey show is world class and the best one I have seen yet in Thailand. The monkeys are trained to scuba dive for coins!

KORAT (โคราช)
Thao Suranaree Victory Celebration Fair (งานย่าโม)

Every year from 23 March to 3 April this fair draws thousands of people from all over Thailand. Khun Ying Mo was the wife of the Governor of Nakhon Ratchasima (Korat) in 1825. Together they initiated the amazing stand to fight off the advancing troops from Laos to protect their homeland.

BURIRAM (บุรีรัมย์)
Pronounced: *(Bù-rii-ram)*

Wat Phanom Rung (วัดพนมรุ้ง) which means "stone castle" is an amazing ancient Khmer temple built somewhere around the 12th century. It is set on the rim of an ancient volcano with an amazing view. The temple was originally a Hindu shrine dedicated to Shiva the Destroyer.

SURIN (สุรินทร์)

Surin is the site of the annual elephant roundup festival held every third week of November. The elephant festival includes an elephant talent show, demonstrations of the various capturing and training techniques as well a presentation of ancient elephant warfare. The end of the show is always set off by the famous tug-of-war between men and elephants. Guess who wins?

KHON KAEN (ขอนแก่น)

Khon Kaen is home to the Khon Kaen National Museum (พิพิธภัณฑสถานแห่งชาติขอนแก่น) and has a diverse selection of archaeological finds from the region. Most of the relics come from the famous archaeology sites at Muang Fa Daet Song Yang and Ban Chiang.

Magnificent temples such as this one are found in Khon Kaen.

PART FIVE

Vocabulary List

a lot *(yér)* เยอะ

airport *(sà-nǎam-bin)* สนามบิน

afraid *(klua)* กลัว

afternoon *(tawn-bàay)* ตอนบ่าย

aircon bus/coach *(rót-thua)* รถทัวร์

airconditioning *(ae)* แอร์

airline *(sǎay-kaan-bin)* สายการบิน

airplane *(krûeang-bin)* เครื่องบิน

airport *(sà-nǎam-bin)* สนามบิน

aisle *(thaang-doen)* ทางเดิน

ambulance *(rót-phá-yaa-baan)* รถพยาบาล

angry *(kròt)* โกรธ

another (want something again) *(ìik)* อีก

apple *(áep-pêrn)* แอปเปิ้ล

April *(may-sǎa-yon)* เมษายน

Are you busy? *(khun wâang-mái)* คุณว่างไหม

area (in the area of) *(thǎew)* แถว

arrive *(thǔeng)* ถึง

ATM card *(bàt-a-thii-em)* บัตรเอทีเอ็ม

ATM machine *(tôu-a-thii-em)* ตู้ เอทีเอ็ม

August *(sǐng-hǎa-khom)* สิงหาคม

aunt *(pâa)* ป้า

available *(wâang)* ว่าง

[B]

backache *(pùat-lǎng)* ปวดหลัง

baht *(bàat)* บาท

banana *(klûay)* กล้วย

Bangkok *(krung-thêp)* (กรุงเทพ)

bank (financial) *(thá-naa-khaan)* ธนาคาร

bathroom *(hâwng-nám)* ห้องน้ำ

beach *(thá-lay)* ทะเล

beautiful *(sǔay)* สวย

bed *(tiang)* เตียง

beef noodle soup *(kǔay-tǐaw-núea)* ก๋วยเตี๋ยวเนื้อ

big *(yài)* ใหญ่

bill (in restaurant) *(chék-bin)* เช็คบิล

bite *(kàt)* กัด

blanket *(phâa-hòm)* ผ้าห่ม

bleeding *(lûeat-àwk)* เลือดออก

board (get on) *(khûen)* ขึ้น

bogie *(tôu)* ตู้

bookstore *(ráan-năng-sŭe)* ร้านหนังสือ

bored *(bùea)* เบื่อ

boyfriend *(faen)* แฟน

breathing problem *(hăay-jai-mâi-àwk)* หายใจไม่ออก

bright *(sà-wàang)* สว่าง

brother—older *(phîi-chaay)* พี่ชาย

brother—younger *(náwng-chaay)* น้องชาย

bus *(rót-may)* รถเมล์

bus-station (city) *(sà-thăa-nii...)* สถานี...

bus-station (local) *(baw-khăaw-săaw/thâa-rót)* บ.ข.ส./ท่ารถ

bus stop *(pâay-rót-may)* ป้ายรถเมล์

business class *(chán-thú-rá-kìt)* ชั้นธุรกิจ

business person *(nák-thú-rá-kìt)* นักธุรกิจ

busy *(mâi-wâang)* ไม่ว่าง

buy *(súe)* ซื้อ

[C]

call *(tho-hăa)* โทรหา

calm, patient *(jai-yen)* ใจเย็น

can *(dâi)* ได้

Can you? *(dâi mái)* ได้ไหม

cannot *(mâi dâi)* ไม่ได้

car *(rót-yon)* รถยนต์

cave *(thâm)* ถ้ำ

chair *(kâo-îi)* เก้าอี้

cheerful *(râa-rerng)* ร่าเริง

chicken and rice *(khâaw-mun-kài)* ข้าวมันไก่

chicken noodle soup *(kǔay-tǐaw-kài)* ก๋วยเตี๋ยวไก่

chicken with cashews *(kài-pàt-mét-má-mûang)*
ไก่ผัดเม็ดมะม่วง

chopsticks *(tà-kìap)* ตะเกียบ

close your eyes *(làp-taa)* หลับ ตา

cloudy *(mii-mêk)* มีเมฆ

cockroaches *(má-laeng-sàap)* แมลงสาบ

coffee *(kaa-fae)* กาแฟ

coffee shop *(ráan-kaa-fae)* ร้านกาแฟ

cold (for drink) *(yen)* เย็น

cold (weather) *(nǎaw)* หนาว

color *(sǐi)* สี

come *(maa)* มา

common cold *(pen-wàt)* เป็นหวัด

company worker *(phá-nák-ngaan) (baw-rí-sàt)*
พนักงานบริษัท

computer/laptop *(cawm-phíew-têr)* คอมพิวเตอร์

consultant *(thîi-prùek-sǎa)* ที่ปรึกษา

cough *(ai)* ไอ

cousin *(yâat)* ญาติ

credit card *(bàt-khre-dìt)* บัตรเครดิต

cut/wound *(phlăe)* แผล

cute *(nâa-rák)* น่ารัก

[D]

dance *(tên)* เต้น

daughter *(lôuk-săaw)* ลูกสาว

day *(wan)* วัน

daytime *(klaang-wan)* กลางวัน

December *(than-waa-khom)* ธันวาคม

delicious *(à-ròy)* อร่อย

depart *(àwk)* ออก

department store *(hâang)* ห้าง

deposit *(fàak-ngern)* ฝากเงิน

diarrhea *(tháwng-sĭa)* ท้องเสีย

different *(ùen)* อื่น

Did you eat yet? *(kin khâaw rúe-yang)* กินข้าวหรือยัง

dining car *(tôu-sà-biang)* ตู้เสบียง

dining out *(thaan-aa-hăan)* ทานอาหาร

direct flight *(thîaw-bin-trong)* เที่ยวบินตรง

discount (can you give?) *(lót dâi-mái)* ลดได้ไหม

dizzy *(wian-hŭa)* เวียนหัว

do *(tham)* ทำ

do not/not *(mâi)* ไม่

Do you know? *(khun róu-jàk... mái)* คุณรู้จักไหม

Do you have? *(mii... mái)* มีไหม

doctor *(măw)* หมอ

dollar *(dawn-lâa)* ดอลลาร์

domestic *(nai-prà-thêt)* ในประเทศ

door *(prà-tou)* ประตู

down *(long)* ลง

drive *(khàp)* ขับ

[E]

early morning *(cháo-tru)* เช้าตรู่

east *(thít-tà-wan-àwk)* ทิศตะวันออก

eat (literally, means "eat rice") *(kin-khâaw)* กินข้าว

economy class *(chán-prà-yàt)* ชั้นประหยัด

elephant *(cháang)* ช้าง

elephant trekking *(khìi-cháang)* ขี่ช้าง

email *(ii-meo)* อีเมล์

engineer *(wít-sà-wá-kawn)* วิศวกร

enjoyable/fun *(sà-nùk)* สนุก

exchange money *(lâek-ngern)* แลกเงิน

exchange rate *(àt-traa-lâek-lâek-ngern)* อัตราแลกเงิน

excited *(tùen-tên)* ตื่นเต้น

express train *(rót-dùan)* รถด่วน

evening *(tawn-yen)* ตอนเย็น

[F]

face *(nâa)* หน้า

family *(khrâwp-khrua)* ครอบครัว

fare *(khâa-tŭa)* ค่าตั๋ว

fast *(rew)* เร็ว

fat *(oûan)* อ้วน

father *(phâw)* พ่อ

February *(kum-phaa-phan)* กุมภาพันธ์

feeling well *(sà-baay-dii)* สบายดี

fever *(pen-khâi)* เป็นไข้

first class *(chán-nùeng)* ชั้นหนึ่ง

flight *(thîaw-bin)* เที่ยวบิน

flood *(nám-thûam)* น้ำท่วม

food *(aa-hăan)* อาหา

food poisoning *(aa-hăan-pen-phít)* อาหารเป็นพิษ

fork *(sâwm)* ส้อม

fresh milk *(nom-sòt)* นมสด

Friday *(wan-súk)* วันศุกร์

fried rice *(khâaw-pàt)* ข้าวผัด

full (eaten enough) *(ìm)* อิ่ม

funny *(tà-lòk)* ตลก

[G]
garden *(sŭan)* สวน

gardening *(tham-sŭan)* ทำสวน

gate *(prà-tou)* ประตู

get frightened *(tòk-jai)* ตกใจ

get off/alight *(long)* ลง

girlfriend *(faen)* แฟน

glass (for drinking) *(kâew)* แก้ว

glasses (vision) *(wâen-taa)* แว่นตา

go *(pai)* ไป

go get *(pai ao)* ไปเอา

go together *(pai-dûay)* ไปด้วย

good (pleasant) *(dii)* ดี

goodbye *(la-kon)* ลาก่อน

Good day *(sà-wàt-dii)* สวัสดี

Good morning *(sà-wàt-dii tawn-cháo)* สวัสดีตอนเช้า

Good night *(fǎn-dii)* ฝันดี

good person *(pen khon-dii)* เป็นคนดี

government official *(khâa-râat-chá-kaan)* ข้าราชการ

Grand Palace *(Phrá Baw-rom Má-hǎa Râat-chá-wang)* พระบรมมหาราชวัง

granddaughter *(lǎan-sǎaw)* หลานสาว

grandson *(lǎan-chaay)* หลานชาย

green sweet curry *(kaeng-khǐaw-wǎan)* แกงเขียวหวาน

greetings *(thakthāi)* ทักทาย

[H]

hairbrush/comb *(wǐi)* หวี

handsome *(làw)* หล่อ

happy *(mii-khwaam-sùk)* มีความสุข [formal];

(dii-jai) ดีใจ [informal]

hardworking *(khà-yǎn)* ขยัน

have *(mii)* มี

headache *(pùat-hǔa)* ปวดหัว

heat *(aa-kàat-ráwn)* อากาศร้อน

heavy *(nàk)* หนัก

Hello *(sà-wàt-dii)* สวัสดี

help *(chûay)* ช่วย

here *(thîi-nîi!)* ที่นี่

hike *(dern-pàa)* เดินป่า

hold hands *(jàp-mue)* จับมือ

hospital *(rong-phá-yaa-baan)* โรงพยาบาล

hot *(ráwn)* ร้อน

hot springs *(nám-phú ráwn)* น้ำพุร้อน

hot tea *(chaa-ráwn)* ชาร้อน

hotel *(rong-raem)* โรงแรม

hour *(chûa-mong)* ชั่วโมง

houseflies *(má-laeng-wan)* แมลงวัน

how *(yang-ngai)* ยังไง

How are you? *(sà-baay-dii mái)* สบายดีไหม

how much *(tháo-rài)* เท่าไร

hug *(kàwt)* กอด

humid *(chúen)* ชื้น

humid weather *(aa-kàat-chúen)* อากาศชื้น

hundred *(nùeng-róy)* หนึ่งร้อย
hundred thousand *(nùeng-sǎen)* หนึ่งแสน
hungry *(hǐw)* หิว
hurt/sore *(jèp)* เจ็บ

[I]
I [male] *(phǒm)* ผม
I [female] *(chǎn)* ฉัน
ice *(nám-khaeng)* น้ำแข็ง
iced tea *(chaa-yen)* ชาเย็น
ill *(mâi-sà-baay)* ผมไม่สบาย
impatient *(jai-ráwn)* ใจร้อน
international *(tàang-prà-thêt)* ต่างประเทศ
Internet café *(ráan-nèt)* ร้านเน็ต
island *(gàw)* เกาะ

[J]
January *(mók-kà-raa-khom)* มกราคม
July *(kà-rá-kà-daa-khom)* กรกฎาคม
June *(mí-thù-naa-yon)* มิถุนายน
jungle *(pàa)* ป่า

[K]
kick *(tè)* เตะ
kind, nice *(jai-dii)* ใจดี
kiss *(jòup)* จูบ

knife *(mîit)* มีด

know (to know) *(róu)* รู้

[L]

lake *(thá-lay-sàap)* ทะเลสาป, *(bueng)* บึง

late evening *(tawn-hŭa-khâm)* ตอนหัวค่ำ

lawyer *(thá-naay-khwaam)* ทนายความ

lazy *(khîi-kìat)* ขี้เกียจ

leave/depart *(àwk)* ออก

lecturer *(aa-jaan)* อาจารย์

left [adj.] *(sáay)* ซ้าย

left side *(thaang-sáay)* ทางซ้าย

lemonade *(nám má-naaw)* น้ำมะนาว

lemon shake *(má-naaw pàn)* มะนาวปั่น

lift hand in the air *(yók-mue)* ยกมือ

light weight *(bao)* เบา

like *(châwp)* ชอบ

listen to music *(fang-phleng)* ฟังเพลง

lost *(lŏng-thaang)* หลงทาง

lots of people *(khon yér)* คนเยอะ

loud noise *(sĭang-dang)* เสียงดัง

lovely/cute *(nâa-rák)* น่ารัก

luggage/baggage *(krà-păo)* กระเป๋า

[M]

make *(tham)* ทำ

mango *(má-mûang)* มะม่วง

many *(mâak)* มาก

March *(mii-naa-kom)* มีนาคม

market *(tà-làat)* ตลาด

May *(phrúet-sà-phaa-khom)* พฤษภาคม

May I have____, please? *(khǎw)* ขอ

mechanic *(châang)* ช่าง

medication/medicine/drug *(yaa)* ยา

meet *(jer)* เจอ

metro bus *(rót-may)* รถเมล์

midnight *(thîang-khuen)* เที่ยงคืน

mild (just right) *(phaw-dii)* พอดี

military person *(thá-hǎaan)* ทหาร

milk *(nom-sòt)* นมสด

million *(nùeng-láan)* หนึ่งล้าน

minced pork dish *(khâaw-pàt-kà-phrao-mǒu)* ข้าวผัดกะเพราหมู

minute *(naa-thii)* นาที

mirror *(krà-jòk)* กระจก

miss (you) *(kít-thǔeng)* คิดถึง

Monday *(wan-jan)* วันจันทร์

money, cash *(ngern)* เงิน

mosquito bites *(yung-kàt)* ยุงกัด

mother *(mâe)* แม่

motorbike taxis *(win-maw-ter-sai)* วินมอเตอร์ ไซค์

mountain *(phou-khǎo)* ภูเขา

movies *(dou-nǎng)* ดูหนัง

movie theater *(rong-nǎng)* โรงหนัง

museum *(phí-phít-thá-phan)* พิพิธภัณฑ์

[N]

name *(chûe)* ชื่อ

naughty *(son)* ซน

nauseous *(khlûen-sâi)* คลื่นไส้

need *(tâwng-kaan)* ต้องการ

nephew *(lǎan-chaay)* หลานชาย

Nice dreams *(fǎn-dii)* ฝันดี

niece *(lǎan-sǎaw)* หลานสาว

night *(tawn-khâm)* ตอนค่ำ

night train *(rót-fai tawn-khâm)* รถไฟตอนเย็น

no *(mâi)* ไม่

non air-con bus *(rót-doi-san-mai-prap-akat)*,
   (rót-phat-lom) รถโดยสารไม่ปรับอากาศ, รถพัดลม

noon *(thîang-wan)* เที่ยงวัน

north *(thít-nǔea)* ทิศเหนือ

not *(mâi)* ไม่

November *(phrúet-sà-jì-kaa-yon)* พฤศจิกายน

number/route/line *(sǎay)* สาย

[O]

October *(tù-laa-khom)* ตุลาคม

office worker *(phá-nák-ngaan)* พนักงาน

one way (ticket) *(thîaw-diaw)* เที่ยวเดียว

open *(pèrt)* เปิด

orange *(sôm)* ส้ม

orange juice *(nám-sôm)* น้ำส้ม

ordinary train *(rót-tham-má-daa)* รถธรรมดา

over here *(tîi-nîi)* ที่นี่

over there *(tîi-nôn)* ที่โน่น

[P]

Pad Thai *(pàt-thai)* ผัดไทย

pants *(kaang-keng)* กางเกง

paper *(krà-dàat)* กระดาษ

pardon me *(khǎw-thôt)* ขอโทษ

parking lot *(thîi-jàwt-rót)* ที่จอดรถ

passenger *(phôu-doy-sǎan)* ผู้โดยสาร

passenger car *(tôu-nâng)* ตู้นั่ง

passport *(nǎng-sǔe-doen-thaang)* หนังสือเดินทาง

pen *(pàak-kaa)* ปากกา

pencil *(din-sǎw)* ดินสอ

pharmacy *(ráan-khǎay-yaa)* ร้านขายยา

phone (cell) *(tho-rá-sàp-mue-thǔe)* โทรศัพท์มือถือ

pillow *(mǎwn)* หมอน

pinch *(yìk)* หยิก

pineapple *(sàp-pà-rót)* สับปะรด

plate *(jaan)* จาน

platform/terminal *(chaan-chaa-laa)* ชานชาลา

play *(lên)* เล่น

play musical instruments *(lên-don-trii)* เล่นดนตรี

please *(ná khá/na khráp)* นะคะ/นะครับ

police officer *(tam-rùat)* ตำรวจ

police station *(sà-thǎa-nii-tam-rùat)* สถานีตำรวจ

polite particle [female] *khá/khâ* คะ/ค่ะ

polite particle [male] *khráp* ครับ

post office *(prai-sà-nii)* ไปรษณีย์

price *(raa-khaa)* ราคา

punch *(tàwy)* ต่อย

[R]

rain *(fǒn-tòk)* ฝนตก

rainy *(fǒn-tòk)* ฝนตก

raise [hand] *(yók-mue)* ยกมือ

rapid train *(rót-rew)* รถเร็ว

rent *(châo)* เช่า

require *(tâwng-kaan)* ต้องการ

reserve *(jawng)* จอง

restaurant *(ráan-aa-hǎan)* ร้านอาหาร

return (ticket) *(pai-klàp)* ไปกลับ

ride a bike *(khìi-jàk-kà-yaan)* ขี่จักรยาน

right [adj.] *(khwǎa)* ขวา

right side *(thaang-khwǎa)* ทางขวา

river *(mâe-nám)* แม่น้ำ

room *(hâwng)* ห้อง

round trip *(pai-klàp)* ไปกลับ

run *(wîng)* วิ่ง

runny nose *(nám-môuk-lǎi)* น้ำมูกไหล

[S]

sad *(sǐa-jai/sâo)* เสียใจ/เศร้า

salesperson *(phá-nák-ngaan khǎay)* พนักงานขาย

Saturday *(wan-sǎo)* วันเสาร์

scared *(klua)* กลัว

school *(rong-rian)* โรงเรียน

seat *(thîi-nâng)* ที่นั่ง

second-class *(chán-sǎwng)* ชั้นสอง

see *(hěn)* เห็น

see you later *(láew-jer-kan)* แล้วเจอกัน

September *(kan-yaa-yon)* กันยายน

service fee/charge *(khâa-baw-rí-kaan)* ค่าบริการ

shampoo *(yaa-sà-phǒm)* ยาสระผม

shirt *(sûea)* เสื้อ

shoes *(rawng-tháo)* รองเท้า

short (height) *(tîa)* เตี้ย

shorts *(kaang-keng khǎa-sân)* กางเกงขาสั้น

shy *(aay)* อาย

sing *(ráwng-phleng)* ร้องเพลง

single (ticket) *(thîaw-diaw)* เที่ยวเดียว

sick/ill *(mâi-sà-baay)* ไม่สบาย

sister—elder *(phîi-sǎaw)* พี่สาว

sister—younger *(náwng-sǎaw)* น้องสาว

sit *(nâng)* นั่ง

size *(khà-nàat)* ขนาด

skillful, good at *(kèng)* เก่ง

skin rash *(pen-phùen)* เป็นผื่น

skytrain (BTS) *(rót-fai-fáa)* รถไฟฟ้า

sleep *(nawn)* นอน

sleep well *(nawn-làp-sà-baay)* นอนหลับสบาย

sleeping car *(tôu-nawn)* ตู้นอน

sleepy *(ngûang-nawn)* ง่วงนอน

slow *(cháa)* ช้า

small *(lék)* เล็ก

smart *(chà-làat)* ฉลาด

smoking *(sòup-bù-rìi)* สูบบุหรี่

snow *(hì-má)* หิมะ

soap *(sà-bòu)* สบู่

socks *(thǔng-tháo)* ถุงเท้า

son *(lôuk-chaay)* ลูกชาย

sore eyes *(jèp-taa)* เจ็บตา

sore throat *(jèp-khaw)* เจ็บคอ

special express train *(rót-dùan-phí-sèt)* รถด่วนพิเศษ

south *(thít-tâi)* ทิศใต้

spicy food *(aa-hăan-pèt)* อาหารเผ็ด

spicy shrimp soup *(tôm-yam-kûng)* ต้มยำกุ้ง

spoon *(cháwn)* ช้อน

stand *(yuen)* ยืน

stomachache *(pùat-tháwng)* ปวดท้อง

stop *(jàwt)* จอด

street *(thà-nŏn)* ถนน

stressed *(khrîat)* เครียด

subway (MRT) *(rót-fai-tâi-din)* รถไฟใต้ดิน

Sunday *(wan-aa-thít)* วันอาทิตย์

sunglasses *(wâen-kan-dàet)* แว่นกันแดด

sunny *(dàet-raeng)* แดดจัด

sweetheart *(thîi-rák)* ที่รัก

sweet and sour chicken *(phàt-prîaw-wăan-kài)* ผัดเปรี้ยวหวานไก่

swimming *(wâay-nám)* ว่ายน้ำ

[T]

table *(tó)* โต๊ะ

take a trip, travel *(pai-thîaw)* ไปเที่ยว

take care *(dou-lae)* ดูแล

tall *(sŏung)* สูง

taxis *(táek-sîi)* แท็กซี่

temple *(wát)* วัด

ten *(sìp)* สิบ

ten thousand *(nùeng-mùen)* หนึ่งหมื่น

Thai boxing *(muay-thai)* มวยไทย

Thank you *(khàwp-khun)* ขอบคุณ

thin, skinny *(phǎwm)* ผอม

third class *(chán-sǎam)* ชั้นสาม

think *(khít)* คิด

thirsty *(hǐw-nám)* หิวน้ำ

throw *(yon)* โยน

thousand *(nùeng-phan)* หนึ่งพัน

Thursday *(wan-phá-rúe-hàt)* วันพฤหัสฯ

ticket *(tŭa)* ตั๋ว

ticket office *(hâwng-khǎay-tŭa)* ห้องขายตั๋ว

time *(way laa)* เวลา

time (What time is it?) *(kìi-mong)* กี่โมง

tired *(nùeay)* เหนื่อย

today *(wan-níi)* วันนี้

toothache *(pùat-fan)* ปวดฟัน

toothbrush *(praeng-sǐi-fan)* แปรงสีฟัน

toothpaste *(yaa-sǐi-fan)* ยาสีฟัน

train *(rót-fai)* รถไฟ

train station *(sà-thăa-nii rót-fai)* สถานีรถไฟ

transfer money *(on-ngern)* โอนเงิน

Tuesday *(wan-ang-khaan)* วันอังคาร

two-row minibus *(rót-sŏng-thăew)* รถสองแถว

[U]

university *(má-hăa-wít-thá-yaa-lai)* มหาวิทยาลัย

unkind, mean *(jai-dam)* ใจดำ

uncle *(lung)* ลุง

up *(khûen)* ขึ้น

[V]

van *(rót-tôu)* รถตู้

vehicle *(rót)* รถ

vomiting *(aa-jian)* อาเจียน

[W]

walk *(dern)* เดิน

want *(yàak/yàak dâi)* อยาก/อยากได้

warm *(òp-ùn)* อบอุ่น

watch *(naa-lí-kaa)* นาฬิกา

water *(nám)* น้ำเปล่า

waterfall *(nám-tòk)* น้ำตก

watermelon *(taeng-mo)* แตงโม

watermelon shake *(taeng-mo-pàn)* แตงโมปั่น

wave hand *(bòk-mue)* โบกมือ

Wednesday *(wan-phút)* วันพุธ

week *(aa-thít)* อาทิตย์

well *(sà-baay-dii)* สบายดี

west *(thít-tà-wan-tòk)* ทิศตะวันตก

wet *(pìak)* เปียก

what *(à-rai)* อะไร

What are you doing? *(khun tham à-rai)* คุณทำอะไร

What is going on? / What's up? *(wâa-ngai)* ว่าไง

when *(mûea-rài)* เมื่อไร

where *(thîi-nǎi)* ที่ไหน

who *(khrai)* ใคร

why *(tham-mai)* ทำไม

WiFi connection *(waay-faay)* วายฟาย

windy *(lom-raeng)* ลมแรง

window *(nâa-tàang)* หน้าต่าง

wink [eye] *(krà-phríp-taa)* กระพริบตา

withdraw (money) *(thǎwn-ngern)* ถอนเงิน

worker on a ship *(lôuk-ruea)* ลูกเรือ

worried *(klûm-jai)* กลุ้มใจ

would like/may I have? *(khǎw)* ขอ

[Y]

you *(khun)* คุณ

NOTES